Beyond Religion One

A few excerpts from 5 STAR reviews on Amazon for
BEYOND RELIGION I

Mr. Kapuscinski has an enormous base of religious, scientific, and mythological knowledge, yet he remains an original thinker. ...the author does a masterful job of infusing his wit and humor into the text to make it an enjoyable read no matter how serious the subject matter.

Ronald Piecuch (Amazon.com)

Beyond Religion I is a fascinating and insightful glimpse into spirituality. ... Stanislaw Kapuscinski's thoughts are exposed here with a brilliant voice... His humor keeps the subject matter light and inviting while his revelations are inspiring and life changing. I highly recommend it!

Ally McMahon (Amazon.com)

A potentially life changing collection of essays. It really opens your eyes beyond the structured confines of conventional religions and shows you the freedom of spirituality.

Lucas M (Amazon.com)

If you have an open mind, there is no way to read this and not feel different when you were done.

Ron Pike (Amazon.com)

...author never preaches, and always injects humor into the text to keep it light and making it an enjoyable read. ...The breadth of knowledge he presents is amazing. He is clearly a master of religious, scientific, and mythological knowledge.

(Donna A. Piecuch USA)

A potentially life changing collection of essays. It really opens your eyes beyond the structured confines of conventional religions and shows you the freedom of spirituality. ...I urge you to read these thought provoking essays for yourself and free your spirituality.

(Jerry M., USA)

Other books by Stanislaw Kapuscinski

DICTIONARY OF BIBLICAL SYMBOLISM
KEY TO IMMORTALITY
DELUSIONS—Pragmatic Realism
VISULIZATION—Creating your own Universe
BEYOND RELIGION Volumes I
BEYOND RELIGION Volumes II
BEYOND RELIGION Volumes III
[Three Collections of Essays on Perception of Reality]

Fiction by Stan I.S. Law
(aka **Stanislaw Kapuscinski**)

Novels

WALL—Love, Sex, and Immortality [Aquarius Trilogy Book One]
PLUTO EFFECT [Aquarius Trilogy Book Two]
OLYMPUS—Of Gods and Men [Aquarius Trilogy Book Three]
YESHUA—Personal Memoir of the Missing Years of Jesus
PETER AND PAUL—Intuitive Sequel to Yeshûa
MARVIN CLARK—In Search of Freedom
GIFT OF GAMMAN
ENIGMA OF THE SECOND COMING
ONE JUST MAN [Winston Trilogy Book One]
ELOHIM [Winston Trilogy Book Two]
WINSTON'S KINGDOM [Winston Trilogy Book Three]
THE PRINCESS
GATE—Things my Mother told Me
ALEC [Alexander Trilogy Book One]
ALEXANDER [Alexander Trilogy Book Two]
SACHA—THE WAY BACK [Alexander Trilogy Book Three]
THE AVATAR SYNDROME [Prequel to the Headless World]
HEADLESS WORLD [Sequel to the Avatar Syndrome]
NOW—BEING AND BECOMING

Short stories

THE JEWEL AND OTHER SHORT STORIES
Sci-Fi Series 1
Sci-Fi Series 2
Cats & Dogs Series

BEYOND RELIGION
I

An Inquiry into the Nature of Being
A Personal View

Stanisław Kapuściński
[aka Stan I.S. Law]

**COLLECTED ESSAYS
VOLUME II**

INHOUSEPRESS, MONTREAL, CANADA

Copyright © Stanislaw Kapuscinski 1997
http://stanlaw.ca
Paperback Edition 2015
All rights reserved. No part of this publication may be reproduced, stored in a retrieval system or transmitted in any form or by any means electronic, mechanical, photocopying, recording or otherwise, without the prior written permission of the publisher.

Published by
INHOUSEPRESS
http://inhousepress.ca

Design and layout
Bozena Happach

ISBN 978-0-9731184-0-7

Paperback Edition 2015
INHOUSEPRESS

For Bozena

*…and other people,
who feel a certain sense of dissatisfaction,
a vague unease, with the orthodox teaching.*

*Beyond the doing right, and doing wrong
there is a field.
I'll meet you there.*

Jalal-ud-Din Rumi

*...when faith requires that he relinquishes
his understanding,
then to have faith becomes just as difficult for the most
intelligent person as it is for the person
of the most limited intelligence,
or it presumably becomes even more difficult
for the former.*

Soren Aabye Kierkegaard
1813 – 1855
CONCLUDING UNSCIENTIFIC POSTSCRIPT
[pg.377]

LIST OF ESSAYS

FOREWORD		7
INTRODUCTION		9

1.	I DON'T BELIEVE IN GOD	How it all started...	13
2.	THE LAST THINGS	On eschatology	19
3.	PHENOMENOLOGY	Comments on "His Holiness"	23
4.	LIFE	On the nature of *nephesh* and *El*	27
5.	POWER	On meaning of corruption	31
6.	BODY AND SOUL	On our identification	35
7.	KNOWINGNESS	On outer and inner knowledge	41
8.	FREEDOM	On responsibility	45
9.	QUALITY CONTROL	From Moses to Deming	49
10.	666	On work ethic	53
11.	CELESTIAL AND OTHER BODIES	On theory and practice	57
12.	THE DEAD, THE LIVING AND THE DYING		61
13.	BEING AND BECOMING		65
14.	THE UNKNOWN	On instinct and intuition	69
15.	I DON'T BELONG		75
16.	DUALITY	On opposing forces	79
17.	CREATIVITY	On the creator, creating and the created	83
18.	OLD AGE?	On the New Age	89
19.	SELF	On id, ego and superego	93
20.	A HORSE OF A DIFFERENT COLOUR	The four horses of the Apocalypse	99
21.	CYCLES	On walking in circles	105
22.	PLEASURE		109
23.	PRAYERS		113
24.	TRADITIONS		117
25.	THE MANY AND THE ONE	On outgrowing our gods	121
26.	THE SHEPHERD AND THE SHEEP	On the three levels of understanding of the Bible	127

List of essays, continued:

27	MYTH AND REALITY	On Christian Creed	131
28	THE CARROT AND THE STICK		
		On heaven and hell	135
29	VANISHING WORLDS	More on illusion of reality	139
30	A STRANGER	An inquiry into human progress	143
31	THE STAGE	On perception of reality	147
32	FAITH	The purpose of faith	151
33	YE ARE GODS	On human potential	155
34	VENGEANCE	On the futility of hatred	159
35	PURPOSE	To be or not to be...	165
36	GENESIS	On the creative method	169
37	THE MESSAGE	(and the Messenger)	175
38.	NECESSITIES	On two modes of existence	179
39	QUESTIONS	On self discovery	183
40	CLONING	On Scottish sheep and cardinals	187
41	MEN AND WOMEN OF EVERY ILK		
		On gays, lesbians and celibates.	191
42	SEX		195
43	PROBLEMS	On challenges and opportunities	199
44	SANCTIFYING	Completeness	203
45	SILENCE		207
46	PARALLEL EVOLUTION	On centrifugal and centripetal forces	211
47	ADAM	On the first and other men	215
48	GRACE	States of consciousness	221
49	SALVATION	The saving of *nephesh*	225
50	EVE	More on the animal soul	231
51	THE UNIVERSAL AND THE PARTICULAR		236
52	BEYOND RELIGION	On evolution of consciousness	241

The essays are offered in chronological order in which they have been created. Volume 1 consists of essays written between November 21, 1996 and May 15, 1997. Some additional notes and/or comments have been added in late autumn 1999.

The dates listed are year/month/day as in 961121

FOREWORD

In my earlier years I used to skip the Foreword to get into the meat of the book, to delve into the mind of the writer, fathom his or her hidden thoughts, perhaps, innermost secrets. I was in error. I have learned since that omitting the foreword was like forgetting to meet the host when entering his house. Surely the rooms are saturated with the presence of him whose very being is, for the most part, held and contained within the space and time by the walls one is entering. Yet to fully understand the dwelling, one must meet the dweller.

My true dwelling is my state of consciousness. It is not my permanent abode, but rather a transient expression of the conditions, that, at any particular moment, have bearing on my awareness of the outside universe. I say outside, because while my haven is both, within and without the reaches of my senses, imagination, or even mind, that which defines my essence is within a realm that is unchangeable, singularly permanent, indestructible. I, no more than a pilgrim, reach out from my haven; perhaps heaven is a better word, and stand in awe of the wonders that surround me.

It is my impressions of these wonders that I wish to share with you. I have no desire to convince anyone of anything, to praise or condemn anyone or anything, though it may seem so, at first. I have as much respect for the state of consciousness you inhabit, at any particular moment, as I have for the universe in which we all find the intimacy of our being. In many ways, the two are inseparable. Furthermore, in most essential ways we are all One; we all look out from our inner sanctum, we enter countless states of consciousness; we observe, experience, learn, and retreat to our City of Peace.

What follows I have variously named thoughts, ideas, essays or even, in my more pompous moments, dissertations. In truth – they are neither. They are little more than one man's way of looking at the world. Neither better nor worse than countless others. I trust my way will add, without detracting, expand without creating new barriers to the spectrum of reality. I offer a viewpoint that, hopefully, eliminates paradoxes. I ask no one to adopt my way of looking at the world. I ask everyone to remember that they, like myself, are unique. It is through boundless diversity that the One Consciousness finds Its expression. I like to think that you and I are indispensable components of the Whole.

***

INTRODUCTION

Many, **many years ago,** perhaps in another lifetime, I've been a reasonably ardent member of an Orthodox Church. My life was secure. I knew that if something went wrong I could always rely on someone to take the blame, and even to give me credit when credit was due. I also wasn't too worried about the distant future. I knew that even if I broke any of the Commandments it wouldn't matter too much. I've been told frequently that I was born a sinner, originally blemished so to speak; but not to worry, Jesus died for my sins, so all would be all right. Just have faith, they said. And then, there was always Confession. Five minutes of discomfort, a few Hail Marys and I was on my merry way to heaven. One day. After I died.

Convenient.

If it weren't for the paradoxes, I'd probably still be nestled among the flock. After all, they were my friends (some still are). I shared their customs, traditions, emotional security. Being a sheep wasn't half-bad. All major decisions regarding the welfare of my soul have been made for me. I could always find a sacerdotal friend who would straighten out the error of my ways. In fact I was encouraged not to think too much. Not good for the soul. Leave it to the experts. Why not? They're paid for it.

Life could have been so easy... except for those glaring paradoxes.

How can God be good and allow wars to happen? How

could Jesus say suffer the little children to come to me and then watch them suffer malnutrition in Africa? Why should we become as little children; sure they're cute, but aren't they also egocentric, irresponsible? How can God be infinitely good and infinitely just – both at the same time? How can a newborn not go to heaven just because some priest arrived too late to sprinkle water on his pate? How can I go to heaven if heaven is within me? Why must I love my enemies if everybody else hates theirs? Why did the soul enter my body?
Should I listen to the church or to the Bible?

I felt stifled. I could no longer breathe inside the thick, musty walls of the ecclesiastical protocol. Limited by statements *ex cathedra*, by the infallibility, by symbols that replaced their original meaning, by ritual that took over from the substance. Perhaps the church was protecting the truth from unholy eyes. My eyes. What of the other billion pairs of eyes? Are they unholy too? And what happened to those who knock; is there no longer anyone at the door? I was no longer prepared to wait to have someone open the door for me – what if they lost the key? But more than anything, I was not prepared to wait until I die – before entering paradise.

And there was more.
There were the biblical statements such as: Ye are gods, Be ye perfect, Whosoever believes in me shall never die.... If I never die, how can I go to heaven? Oxymoron? I spent one year reading the Bible. End to end. I became aware of the poetry, of the enticing charm of biblical symbolism, of the incredible source of knowledge. Strangely, I've learned nothing about dying. Only how to live. How to rejoice in the gift of life, perhaps forever. I also grew seriously fed up with all the paradoxes. Einstein said that God didn't play dice with the universe. Well, I considered myself part of the universe. If God had a plan for the universe, I wanted to know what it was. Somewhere the Bible claimed that I've been created in

God's image. Perhaps if I studied the image, I might also learn something about God. And that's when my journey really started.

I asked myself the seemingly simple question:
Who am I?

It seems to me that we are all pilgrims. The ideas that follow are stages in my own journey. Some later insights may even contradict some of the previous ones. This is the excitement of travel. As the scenery changes, our understanding gains a new, perhaps greater perspective. I was moving from the known into the unknown. I continue to do so. I've discovered that often the fastest way to travel is to keep very still. Paradox? No. You'll see. Many of you may have passed this way a long time ago. Still others may not have reached this or that particular mile. A few among you will recognize the twists and turns in my road. It is not always easy to stay on the straight and narrow. Some of you might even enjoy taking the journey with me. If you do, I shall no longer be alone.

Nor will you.

***

*".... the Kingdom is within you, and it is without you.
If you will know yourselves,
then you will be known and will know that you are the sons
of the Living Father.
But if you do not know yourselves,
then you are in poverty and you are poverty."*

THE GOSPEL ACCORDING TO THOMAS
Logion 3.

---

[1] Text translated by A Guillaumont, H.-Ch.Puech, G.Quispel, W.Till and Yassah 'Abd Al Masih [Harper & Row 1959] See also KEY TO IMMORTALITY by Stanislaw Kapuscinski

1

I DON'T BELIEVE IN GOD

We **were walking hand in hand.** The sun cut obliquely intensifying the hues of the sprawling oaks ablaze in their autumnal finery. The maples, drenched to overflowing with gold, lined the broad, winding alley of the Mount Royal Park. Overhead the sky rivalled the purest azure of the southern Adriatic. It was a day of glory, designed to saturate me with warmth, to take me through the Canadian winter. A day to remember – filled with hope. Amid such beauty the divine presence was really palpable. It was all around us. It filled me with awe, serenity. We chatted distractedly, inhaling the sweet fragrance of fall. I felt like composing a psalm of praise – of gratitude. I said as much.

"I don't believe in God," she said.

I fell silent. Speechless is a better word. Could it be that the woman with whom I have spent a dozen years, whom I thought I knew well enough to read her thoughts, didn't believe in the evidence of her own eyes? Were we not both staring at the very same, direct manifestation of infinite Beauty, Life, Benevolence...

I found it difficult to talk after that. I tried to dismiss her statement from my mind. It wouldn't go. It kept gnawing at the corners of my awareness. It was jagged, raspy. Painful. Could I have misunderstood? I didn't dare to ask. Had she said it looking at some TV pictures of war atrocities, at the starving children of Africa, at the first page of our daily newspaper – I would have understood. But here? In heaven, the absence of God is too ludicrous to contemplate.

It took me some time to understand.

At home I looked up my Webster. The dictionary states the following:

god, a. and n. good (Obs.)

And then it hit me. (Obs.) meaning: obsolete. The meaning of god or God and good or the infinite Good is now obsolete. It's a pity, I thought. A great pity. I wondered what is it that people believe in these-days. Money? Sex? Drugs, murder and mayhem so vividly expressed by our media entertainment? Maybe some did, but surely, not she! We talked about God before but always inconclusively. It is not easy to be conclusive about God. As difficult as being personal about the Impersonal. And for a hundredth time I wondered, what is it that she really believes in. Can anyone really know what another believes?

There is hardly one amongst us who will not deny identifying god with an ancient, gray-bearded Man, whose stern yet fatherly features seem ever willing to reward or punish us for our actions. An anthropomorphic god. A god created by man in man's image and likeness. We, the advanced 20th century men and women, do not ascribe to such primitive, childish fantasies. We are past such primitive concepts. We are much too sophisticated.

Yet in moments of trouble, especially dire trouble, we bend our knees and beg god for forgiveness. We offer sacrifices – a mending of our ways. We ask for his help, his mercy, his fatherly concern. The long, gray beard reappears as if by magic. We are, once again, his children, helpless, unable to cope with the life we have created for ourselves. It is abundantly evident, that deep – at the subconscious level –

this fatherly, albeit all-powerful and, surely, loving-if-stern image still persists. And if, in spite of our intellectual assurances, we did not relinquish such a concept of god, than such an image will continue to govern our reality. Why? Because god or God is whatever we truly believe He, She or It is. He, She or It is a compendium of traits which we, the believers, assign to It; and whatever it is, this image, concept, illusion shall govern our tiny subjective universe, in which all things happen as we deeply perceive they should. Or shouldn't. Depending on our belief.

To define God is to deny God, averred a mystic philosopher named Spinoza. Had he been right? Probably. Or does an image of God change over the centuries? Does it grow with our understanding of It? Does it expand in direct proportion to the expansion of our consciousness? In 1656 Baruch Spinoza had been excommunicated from the Jewish group in which he was raised for daring to create his own image of god. He dared to insist that all is One, that All is God. Mind, matter, time, our dreams, desires, you and me... all that is perceptible is but a manifestation of the One. He also insisted that God is Good. That evil exists only for the *finite* mind but has no substance when seen as part of the Whole.

Not bad for a lack of definition.

So much for One. But what of a *personal* god. One hears so much about such a Being lately. We hear of people having a personal relationship with a personal god. Well, why not? As long as they do not limit their personal god too much, but make Him, Her or It reasonably omnipotent. To make Himherit good. As good as they can imagine. Because if they imagine that their god will punish them – Hesheit will. To the extent and degree that the believer commands. *According to your faith be it unto you*[2]. This could prove positively dan-

---

[2] Matthew 9:29

gerous.

Emmet Fox, writing almost extensively on Biblical subjects, found a reasonable way out. He put together a list of traits that he needed his God to possess. He called these traits Aspects. While, like Spinoza, he would not presume to limit God to a specific number of traits (in fact saying that the number is infinite), Fox identified, what he called, the Seven Main Aspects of God.[3] Every one of us can go through such an exercise and list our own aspects, which we shall (and invariably do) assign to our God. Why? The First Book of Kings explains it as follows: "And I will take thee, and thou shalt reign *according to all that thy soul desireth,* and shalt be king over Israel."[4] *Whatever* your soul desires. Whatever you decide shall rule your consciousness (Israel, your kingdom, your reality). Your life. The Book of Proverbs states: *as he thinketh in his heart, so (is) he*.[5] "Whatsoever you think that I am, that I shall be unto you." This is what my Lord is saying to me. I have to watch my thoughts!

Today it is safe to assume that the word god (with or without a capital G) became a euphemism for whatever we choose to assign power to. Throughout history the churches, kings and other authoritarians used the word "god" to usurp absolute power over those they managed to fool into submission. Some continue to do so today. Or at least to try. It seems that many of us are still in need of that kindly-if-stern-fatherly-figure to whom we can run for succour, to whom we can turn in trouble, whom we can blame for our misfortunes. Such are the Hebrew and the Christian gods. At least to most believers I've met. They are dualistic gods. They are invariably blamed for both, the good and the bad in our lives. They

---

[3] Fox, Emmet ALTER YOUR LIFE [Harper and Row, New York]

[4] (3rd after the reckoning from the titles in Jerome's Latin Vulgate) I Kings 11:37.

[5] Proverbs 23:7

reward and punish. Indeed the Webster definition is obsolete. God no longer means Good. Did it ever?

Or perhaps we are only beginning to reach the level of understanding to give the old meaning its full impact. Perhaps we are ready to stand on our hind legs and become responsible for our actions, our words, our thoughts. Perhaps we are ready to create a god in our consciousness that will be synonymous with Good, with divine Good, with perfect ideal of Life, of infinite Beauty, of unlimited, divine Love. When we do learn to believe in such a God we shall take the first step towards being reborn unto His image and likeness. Or Her image and likeness. Whatever we decide He or She or It is in our hearts.

The next day we walked the park again. Nothing had changed.

And then I noticed that whenever I looked at someone approaching us from the opposite direction they were smiling. I thought it might be the autumn colours. But then, as they neared us, I tried to follow their eyes. I noticed that those total strangers invariably seemed to steal glances at my wife. The unbeliever. Oh, she's beautiful enough, but... it wasn't that. I began to steal glances at her myself. Unobtrusively, sideways.

Soon I too smiled – my understanding. When least expecting it, I discovered the first two of the traits that my god shall have. They will be Love and Life. These two, when mixed in the sparkling cauldron of her eyes, were blended into Joy. Joy which those gazing at her couldn't resist. And they smiled.

***

961121

*"The point is not to gain some knowledge about philosophy
but to be able to philosophize.
....Phenomenology is the name for the method of ontology,
that is, of scientific philosophy.
Rightly conceived,
phenomenology is the concept of a method."*

Martin Heidegger
1889 – 1976
[THE BASIC PROBLEMS OF PHENOMENOLOGY]

2

THE LAST THINGS

Reading the book entitled HIS HOLINESS,[6] I came across a strange statement. The authors claim that Karol Wojtyła, the future pope, became so preoccupied with the untimely death of his brother that the "Last Things", or subjects dealing with the apocalyptic accounts in the Bible, took over his consciousness. The Four Last Things are listed in this order: death, judgement, heaven, and hell.[7]

At fourteen years of age, as he then was, Karol Wojtła had been already greatly influenced by the Catholic Church. He attended mass daily, often dropped in to the church after school. He certainly took his religion extremely seriously and thus must have been under considerable influence of the Church's teaching. It is evident that after being dealt such painful blows,[8] his turning to the "Last Things" was a desperate cry for help, a search for justice, understanding, perhaps a reaching out for solace, compassion.

---

[6] HIS HOLINESS by Carl Bernstein and Morco Politi, subtitled: "John Paul II and the Hidden History of Our Time" [Doubleday, New York, 1996] pg. 27.

[7] The Catholic Encyclopedia calls the subjects dealing with the 'Last Things' Eschatology.

[8] His mother died when he was 8, and apparently there had been a sister whom he never knew. The brother, whom Karol idolized and adored, died when the future pope was 14.

Under the circumstances the order in which the Last Things are listed take on an ominous air. One can only imagine the influence that such dire, morbid subjects must have had on a young, impressionable personality. Imagine being deeply saddened, perhaps on the verge of depression, and having to face, alone, the dark finality of death and judgment, and even greater finality heaven and hell. I must stress here, again, that it is not Karol's untimely evocative interests that disturbed me, but the order in which, the young, teenage mind was compelled to face them.

I have scoured the Bible to find substance to such a dismal order of this eschatological doom. I could not find it. The Bible talks of the last days, but does so with joy. Micah talks of the last days as those in which: "*...the mountains of the house of the LORD shall be established in the top of the mountains, and* (that) *it shall be exalted above the hills: and* (that) *people shall flow unto it.*"[9]

Now since people do not flow *up* mountains, this phrase is a dead give-away that we are dealing (as so very often in the scriptures) with an allegory. Students of biblical symbolism are well aware that mountains, in the Bible, invariably stand for a state of raised consciousness. The LORD stands for the divine presence of the Infinite within us. Nowadays references to the Lord have been translated as the Higher Self, the Immortal Spark, or the El (as in Is-Ra-El) of the Old Testament. The prophet Micah assures us that the last days shall only take place when we shall arrive at the highest state of awareness, perhaps the Christ consciousness, and that this illustrious state shall be exalted to such a degree that people shall be drawn (shall flow) towards It.

Note that there is nothing sad or worrisome about the last days. On the contrary, such a condition shall be exalted! Could this be what drew young Karol to this subject?

---

[9]   Micah 4:1

In the New Testament, Jesus says: *"...that of all which he* (the Father in heaven) *hath given me I should lose nothing, but should raise it up again at the last day.*[10] As usual, Jesus talks about the soul. The *all which he hath given me* are the indestructible states of consciousness, the immortal aspects which all of us entertain within us but so few appear to identify with. That which we really *are* cannot be lost, injured or destroyed. It knows no death, bar that of a temporary illusion of a separation from the Truth. We are admonished to raise our consciousness to the higher level of understanding in which we shall identify with that within us which is immortal. If *all* that is good (which came from the Father) shall be raised on the *last day*, then we are not some physical beings interacting with our sinful egos. We are immortal entities interacting with a material substance of our physical bodies. Our ego is what sets us apart; our soul is what unifies us with the Infinite. Is this what the precocious teenager found in his hour of need?

It could not have been easy for Karol. Then and now people have difficulties understanding the true reality. The prophets and Jesus devoted their lives trying to explain this simple truth. Yet Paul, in his letter to the Romans, seems sad when he refers to the Old Testament saying: *"There is none that understandeth, there is none that seeketh after God"*.[11] Jesus too calls on Isaiah, quoting: *"By hearing ye shall hear, and shall not understand; and seeing ye shall see, and shall not perceive."*[12] Later Jesus sounded even more despondent: *"why do ye not understand my speech?"* he cried.[13]

---

[10] John 6:39-4
[11] 4:11
[12] Matthew 13:14, Isaiah 6:9
[13] John 8:43

But let us attempt to rearrange the order of the "Last Things". Let us list them as heaven and hell and death and judgement. If we were to regard heaven and hell as *states of consciousness*, heaven being the raised, the exalted condition (the mountain) and hell the barren desert, an illusory feeling of separation from the Whole (i.e. God), then what joy would we experience when the latter were to "die" and we reverted to the joy of the awareness of Oneness. After all, from the top of the mountain we enjoy unlimited horizons. As for judgement – this, surely, is an exercise we practice not only as a "last thing" but daily. We practice discrimination, directing our thoughts toward ever-higher "mountains". Such *last* things would not hurt young Karol. They would give him solace indeed.

There are things that may come last, which are final. But not for soul. As soul we are immortal. The young Karol must have known that.

Or perhaps discovered it – just then.

***

961120

3

PHENOMENOLOGY

This complex word is defined in the Webster dictionary as the science dealing with phenomena, as distinct from the science of being (ontology[14]). Webster also offers a definition of the word phenomenalism as the philosophic theory that knowledge is limited to phenomena, either because there is no reality beyond phenomena or because such reality is unknowable. The root of both words – phenomenon – (from Greek *phainomenon*, ppr. of *phainesthai*, to appear) is defined as (inter alia) any fact, circumstance, or experience that is apparent to the senses and that can be scientifically described or appraised, and, the appearance or observed features of something experienced as distinguished from reality or the thing in itself.

The Columbia Viking desk Encyclopedia defines Phenomenology as a modern school of philosophy founded by Edmund Husserl, who tried to develop a universal philosophic method focusing only on visible phenomena. The method demands suspension of all preconceived judgments in order to elucidate the meaning of what is observed through

---

[14] To be more precise, ontology (from Greek *ontos*, ppr. of *einai*, to be) is the branch of metaphysics dealing with the nature of being or reality.

intuition.[15]

Imagine my surprise when reading *His Holiness*,[16] a book dealing with the life and times of Karol Wojtyla (later pope John Paul II), I learned that His Holiness not only subscribed to this philosophy, but also wrote two books on the subject. The first in Polish: *Osoba i Czyn* and the second in English which started as a translation of the Polish version, but thanks to a deep involvement and editing by Dr. Anna-Teresa Tymieniecka, it became an authoritative statement of the popes philosophy. This latter book is entitled *The Acting Person*.

Let me confess at once that heretofore I read neither of the books though I intend to satisfy my curiosity at the first opportunity. Whatever the papal interpretation of the modern philosophy of phenomenology however, one thing is certain. This new science is almost by definition in direct opposition to Thomism, the teaching of St. Thomas Aquinas, on whose *Summa Theologica* the Church based its promulgation since the thirteenth century.

[I shall not attempt to dive headlong into the St. Thomas's scholasticism which attempted to reconcile the Aristotelian thought with the Christian faith. Nor shall I regress to the 4th century B.C. to discuss the deductive rather than inductive and experimental rather than intuitive method of arriving at conclusions. Aristotle, the most prominent pupil of Plato, was sufficiently prolific in his analyses].

Within the context of phenomenological philosophy, what interests me is a single statement attributed to Jesus. 1300 years before St. Thomas and some 325 after the death of Aristotle Jesus said: *I and my Father are one*.

---

[15] Gleamed from the Columbia Viking desk Encyclopedia, [Viking Press] Third Edition.

[16] HIS HOLINESS by Carl Bernstein and Marco Politi; [Doubleday, New York]. (see above)

A phenomenal statement?

As is usual with biblical statements, one is forced to assume that the quotation is not to be taken literally. I must say I have a hidden admiration for some fundamentalist sects that manage to contrive a literal meaning to allegoric reflections. Let us agree that Jesus did not claim to be one with St. Joseph, his "earthly" father, nor was he referring to any other *phenomenal* male who may have been instrumental in his incarnation.

Since Jesus did mention, on quite a number of occasions, that to perceive the true reality (which will set us free) we must be born of Spirit,[17] it is safe to assume that Jesus was referring to his *spiritual* rather than biological progenitor, and that, therefore, his *Father* is synonymous with the Spirit. Under the circumstances, can we regard the spirit in a phenomenal context? Can we regard the spirit as an observable phenomenon?

Once again, almost by definition, we cannot. After all, if spirit were observable by or through our senses, it would no longer be spirit. It would be matter/energy. Apparently we must suspend the Webster definition of phenomenon – *circumstance, or experience that is apparent to the senses and that can be scientifically described or appraised* – as well as phenomenology – *as the science dealing with phenomena.* We are left either with a paradox, or must defer to a stipulation of the greatest (if fictional) of all detectives.

Mr. Sherlock Holmes said (something to the effect) that if in any given circumstances all the solutions (the tangible, observable phenomena) prove impossible then the residual alternative, no matter how seemingly improbable, must be the true solution. And what would that solution be? Jesus supplies us with the answer. He said quite clearly that he and his Father are one. He and the spirit are one. Ergo: there is no matter. There is no physical universe as such. The universe is

---

[17] John 3:5-7 et al., and John 8:32

composed of spirit and spirit alone. What we see as phenomenal events or objects are really an illusion. The true and the only reality is Spirit.

Though this also might sound rather farfetched, St. Paul attempts to provide us with an inkling of true reality. He says: now *we see through a glass, darkly...*[18] Apparently we are attempting to collect illusory phenomenal data with illusory eyes, ears, senses, instruments. But the lens distorts reality. The glass itself is not real. The only true senses are those of our spiritual body. None other can give us the truth. *Vanity of vanities, saith the Preacher, vanity of vanities: all is vanity.*[19]

Vanity, illusion, a truth distorted beyond recognition.

The phenomenal world is an illusion.

It does not really exist. The atoms, within whatever our physical senses fool us as perceiving, are in a constant state of flux. They are bundles of energy whirling within a matrix of forces beyond the capability of our instruments to measure. The spaces between the atoms in solid objects are, in proportion, so wide as the distance between the physical earth and the physical sun. What we really perceive with out empty eyes is empty space. All is vanity.

There is no physical universe. What we see with our illusory senses is but a shadow cast by the True Reality. We alone are real. But we are spiritual beings. Whether we know it or not.

***

961120

---

[18] I Corinthians 13:12

[19] Ecclesiastes (or the Preacher) 1:2

4

LIFE

How important is life? Great ecclesiastic dignitaries assure us that human life is the most sacred of all. Leaders, in an effort to guide people who are at the stage of development that requires guidance, add such prerequisites as dignity, equality, well-being, and an adequate level of financial security. Apparently we all have an inalienable right (although no one with the exception of Ayn Rand mentions at whose expense)[20] to employment, education, free medical care, pensions, a roof over our heads and enough to eat to make us at least reasonably unhealthy. All to enhance our life.

Most sacred life, of course.

Presumably to make sure that we do not overindulge in this Edenic euphoria, the pope, for instance, demands of us (to whom this may apply) unquestioning obedience. He demands this obedience while insisting that other leaders (presidents, dictators and disparate heads of other misguided faiths and political systems) must give us absolute freedom, so that we might obey him (and him only) absolutely. A paradox? Not according to His Holiness. We are assured that all this is so as to improve the physical not to mention moral quality of our life. Perhaps. But before we accept the precepts

---

[20] VIRTUE OF SELFISHNESS by Ayn Rand [Signet Books, New York] Ms. Rand points out that we have a right to pursue certain benefits – not be given such at other people's expense.

of all the infallible paragons of virtue, there seem to be a tiny little question that begs to be answered:

What is life?

Some claim that life begins at the moment of conception. Sperm winds its murky way toward an unsuspecting egg, a tiny puncture and bingo, we have life. Others say that life is only manifest when the (human) cranium appears in the outside world and the baby takes its first breath. But how did the baby get there? That's an easy one. There was a cell which divided into two cells, which divided into two cells each, which... rather like a single bacterium which in a mere eight hours can merrily divide to produce 1,000,000,000 bacteria.[21] That's right, one billion. All in a day's work. Talk of life! Of course, according to some religious authorities this life doesn't matter. It is not sacred; it is not human.

Convenient.

The baby eats, defecates, sleeps, crawls, walks, and grows. It, the grown up baby, walks *on* and *in* its own offal. No, it no longer needs the security of diapers; he/she is trained now, rather like my kitten – only it took a lot longer. Nevertheless it does walk in its own biological waste. How? As it walks, every hour it sheds around 1.5 million dead skin flakes. We recognize them as dust on our floors. But not to worry. A veritable army of insatiable mites spends their entire existence eating up bits and pieces of our dead, dried-up pieces of skin. Epidermal delight. The more we shed, the more they eat... and multiply. Our loss is their gain. But although they save us from eventual drowning in the dead cells of our own bodies, their life is not sacred either. I suppose they are a little like domestic help in some illustrious residences of our social elite. Sub-human?

---

[21] Most scientific data have been gleamed from the NOVA program called the Odyssey of Life, aired on channel 33, on 96.11.25.

Is life a biological infestation? Is there life in our organs, brain, heart, blood, cells? Are we impregnated with it? Are we alone imbued with this *sacred* cycle of life that so diligently omits all other biological forms?

Are we alone?

Certainly not physically. We live in great togetherness. Not with other people. With them – we fight. We live in relative harmony with some 100,000 billion microbes. For the more mathematically minded this figure looks like this: 100,000,000,000,000 or 10^{14}. We are permanent hosts to this congregation. Without them we would die. That is to say, our biological functions would cease. We are at the mercy of vermin. But they are not sacred either. And worse. We are also hosts to hosts of viruses – pieces of genetic material surrounded by protein. Lately the scientists have added "preeons", pieces of protein which, contrary to bacteria, viruses and protozoa, do not even need DNA to divide and multiply.

Do they all want to live?

And then there are parasites. They seem to attack the sacred human and the unholy animals alike. No preferential treatment is accorded. Parasites are responsible for more death than any other organism.

So what makes us, humans, so sacred? We are a battlefield on which the viruses, the bacteria and our immune system are engaged in a battle to the death. Eat or be eaten. There is no mercy in this world of which we seem to be such an integral part. We – the sacred cows of religious powerhouses. To my knowledge, most religions acclaim us to be superior to whatever we come in contact with. Even if we can't even see it. Even if it kills us with the ease of a microscopic virus.

Is this really life?

Or is life something which has nothing to do with any of the above?

Is life not at all a biological infestation, be it of viral, bacterial, parasitic or of human variety? At the biological level, we all eat, defecate, multiply, kill with no mercy. All of us, including the sacred cows. Perhaps more so. We, humans, kill even when we are not hungry. Just for pleasure. For sport.

I wish those looking after our moral and ethical welfare would stop worrying. That, within us, which is sacred, is also present in all other biological manifestations. It is also present in the trees and flowers, in the air we breath. The rocks and the sand are saturated with It. The visible universe is a manifestation of Its invisible presence. Life is an integral, indivisible part of the Whole. The awareness of this Oneness manifests itself as Soul. It, and It alone, is sacred. It is also indestructible, immortal, and omnipresent. No human agency, no matter how "sacred" can injure It in any way whatever. So... do not worry so much about Life.

If you believe in this one, last paragraph, you'll never die.

***

961123

A conscious, passionate, single-minded intensity
tends to dampen out ambiguity and achieve a realization...
We are finally confronting the mirror of our true selves...
We are in our own hands.

Joseph Chilton Pearce
[22]

---

[22] THE CRACK IN THE COSMINC EGG [Washington Square Press, New York 1971] pg. 184

5

POWER

I know of few people who are not acquainted with the phrase: "power corrupts, absolute power corrupts absolutely". More often than not we cite this expression without analyzing its deeper meaning. Why does power corrupt? Were all our kings and princes, our presidents and ministers, popes and bishops, mullahs and preachers, judges and advocates and other men and women wielding power... corrupt? If so how does this corruption manifest itself?

What is power, anyway?

In physics power is the energy made capable of doing work. In mechanics it is that which tends to produce motion. In engineering, power is the energy of all kinds taking different forms such as mechanical or electrical. In mathematics it is a sort of inverse of a root. In optics it is the degree of magnification. It is also the ability to act, to react, to conduct oneself in an autonomous manner. I do not believe that any of the above tend to corrupt.

We associate power with birthright, prerogative, privilege, right, management, ascendancy, dominance, dominion, sovereignty, influence, prestige, force, strength... we are beginning to tread on dangerous ground. Power is also synonymous with authority, command, control, domination, jurisdiction, mastery, might, strings, sway, supremacy, superiority...

leading directly to corruption of one who practices such on one's neighbour. But only *leading* to corruption. After all, there are many who wish to be lead, who need to be controlled or at least restrained, who wish to live under the jurisdiction of a powerful Authority. And one may also wish to exercise mastery over one's own weaknesses.

Still, we are now walking on very dangerous ground. There is a distinct suction heard as we steer our boots laden with self-righteousness through the quagmire.

The corruptive influence of power is not in how we apply it towards others, but what it does to us. To our psyche. It riles the waters, it distorts our vision, pollutes our soul. Why? Surely I exercise power (physical strength, will power, power of decision, overcoming fear) as I lift a baby which falls, inadvertently, in front of an oncoming truck. It is also within my power to forgive, to atone, to help – when requested. We also heard about the power of love.

That last is an oxymoron. Power is the opposite of love. Even as Absolute Power is the opposite of Unconditional Love.

The corruptive influence of power applies only to the kind, the noble, the saintly. The others are already corrupt. They have nothing to lose, so to speak. But the goodly, those who firmly desire to do so much for so many – they are in danger. No matter what the effort, what sacrifice. Those who are willing, and sometimes able to sacrifice their very lives to do good unto others... they are the victims of power.

There is one ethical axiom that can save us from the wiles of power: The end does *not* justify the means. Ever.

No matter how noble the intention, how wonderful our hopes, how altruistic, how prodigious the apparent benefits... the end does *not* justify the means. And those who wield power are in a position to sacrifice more means than those who do not.

A practical example comes to mind. A man wants to do good for others. He is honest, hardworking, altruistic. (Good enough to be corrupted). He gets elected to the parliament. After the statutory period in power, new elections are called. The man, the good, honest, hardworking man is halfway through his program. If he does not get re-elected, the chances are great that the program he initiated will be shelved. He has put in four years of self-denial, sleepless nights, and hard labour, to have his program accepted by his party. He worked so hard his wife left him; his children hate his guts. He sacrificed everything. (Did I mention he was driven by altruism?)

Now come the elections. If he accepts money from unclean sources he can augment his advertising campaign. His chances for re-election shall increase exponentially. He would not do it for himself. He would do it for the cause. A great cause. He cannot do more himself. He already gave his all. He accepts the money. He doesn't keep one cent for himself. He buys the votes. Indirectly, of course.

The man compromised his principles. His program was designed to clean up corruption. On the election night, on the way to the local party headquarters, the once noble man falls under a truck.

Power first proposes, then imposes, finally forces us to obey. "For our own good", of course. It takes away our freedom of choice, offers to do our thinking for us, lowers our resistance until we succumb to it. Power corrupts our minds, our ability to be individuals, to respect individuality; but mostly it corrupts the one exercising such power over others. You must be noble before you can be corrupted. Corruption is another word for compromise. Both jeopardize ethics. The greater the compromise the greater the corruption. As I mentioned before, power is the opposite of love. You can always compromise on power, never on love. You can give the citizen some freedom; you cannot give them only a little love. Love is indivisible.

Have you heard? Compromise is said to be the soul of politics.

***
961123

*Society in every state is a blessing,
but government in its best state
is but a necessary evil,
in its worst state, an intolerable one.*

Thomas Paine
1737 – 1809
[COMMON SENSE]

6

BODY AND SOUL

Few of us have any problems** identifying with our bodies. These physiological structures have this amazing arsenal of senses that enable them, that is us, to distinguish and experience other bodies. They, the bodies, also move us around. They give us pleasure. They also give us pain. They come in various shapes and sizes: tall or short, thin or fat, healthy or decrepit. They seem to formulate and define our tiny, subjective universes. Yes, we definitely identify ourselves with our physical enclosures.

Soul is quite another problem. The Old Testament, the Torah, refers to the soul as *nephesh*,[23] which means "animal soul". In the same scriptures a woman invariably symbolizes a soul, but this time she represents the subconscious (as well as our feeling nature). Carl Jung referred to the subconscious as the animus (positive) and anima (negative) which help to balance our positive (active or male) and negative (passive or female) minds or psyches. In other words, "passive" women

---

[23] The Hebrew word *nephesh* is invariably translated as soul, meaning animal soul or the sub-conscious. When the word for spirit is needed, the Hebrews used *neshamah* (Isiah 57:16), meaning *breath* which prompted some to suggest that the spirit enters the baby only when it takes its first breath. The same is true of the Greek word pneuma (from *pneim*: to breathe) variously translated as the breath of life, spirit or soul.

are imbued with "active" subconscious, and the men the other way round. Since we all claim that the conscious state is the one controlling our life on earth, the man is assigned the active or the ruling role, with the woman being passive or subservient. This symbolic treatment, however, suggest that the tip of the iceberg (the conscious mind) controls the submerged part (the subconscious). We all know that is nonsense but, apparently, that is the way it's *supposed* to be. We are supposed to live conscious lives; not be guided by subconscious whims resulting from an ocean of instinctual baggage. Although men and women each enjoy male and female characteristics, neither, with few exceptions, achieved the state of full conscious living. Such an achievement would be described as Cosmic Consciousness, when the conscious and the subconscious become one.

[In this context, the word "cosmic" refers to the microcosm, i.e. the subjective world we live in].

But, there is more to it than that?

Or at least there is more to the concept of Cosmic Consciousness than the marriage of the conscious and the subconscious. While, more often than not, the Bible refers to the subconscious as the soul, there is also a reference to the *spiritual* aspect of the human psyche. The name *Israel* is the key to this condition. *Is* represents the subconscious / feminine aspect of our nature, *RA* the conscious/male, and *El* the spiritual or universal aspect of the human entity. Apparently only when we become *fully* aware of having the *El* component, we begin our conscious journey towards our true Self. When Jesus told a man to let the *dead* bury their dead[24], he was re-

---

[24] Matthew 8:22. I recall a story about imparting esoteric knowledge. A man has been told to love his enemies. He left the feet of his Master looking very unhappy. He came back later all smiles. "What makes you so happy?" the Master asked. "Well," said the man, "I had no enemies. When I left your feet, Master, I went out and hit the first man I saw on the mouth. He became my sworn enemy. Now I have someone to love."

ferring to those Jews who have not, as yet, become aware of their spiritual nature.

This awareness, according to the symbolism of the Bible, is the secret of success. From the evolutionary standpoint, we begin our lives as animals. All of us. We differ from other animals only in the degree to which we can manipulate matter. But a monkey differs from an amoeba a lot more than most of us differ from a monkey. It's all relative. Biologically, the differences spring from the complexity of organism. The more complex – the more advanced. A present-day supersonic jet is more advanced than a biplane of the first world war. The memory of a jet's computer banks is staggering. One might call it the subconscious – the operating system being the conscious component, though it only reacts to its sensors. But a computer is not aware of its spiritual nature. In the biblical sense it is dead – as are men and women who do no more than react to their programming. As mentioned before, not only human species walks on the two hind legs. So does an ostrich. What makes us different from other animal forms is our *capacity* to come alive. To become aware of our spiritual nature. Prophet Isaiah described the birth of this higher awareness as follows: "For unto us a child is born, unto us a son is given: and the government shall be upon his shoulder: and his name shall be called Wonderful, Counsellor, The mighty God, The everlasting Father, The Prince of Peace". [25]

And this is the key.

This Higher consciousness is our true domain. This consciousness is not only Wonderful, but it is indivisible from the spirit (the mighty God, the everlasting Father), it is one with the Christ Consciousness (the Prince of Peace). It is an awareness that we, by our ultimate birthright, are immor-

---

[25] Isaiah 9:6

tal, indestructible, incorruptible components of the Whole. Each one of us, as individuals[26], are indivisible from the Whole.

When one human sperm in 500,000,000 is allowed through the egg membrane, an animal with a potential is conceived. An *animal* with a potential. The cells know what to do. They divide. A blastula is formed: several layers of cells around a central cavity forming a hollow sphere. A rudimentary embryo. The cells continue to divide automatically. After three months it becomes a foetus: a name given to an animal embryo (including human) in its later phases of gestation. At this stage (and for another few months) a human embryo has fewer brain cells than a monkey. The automatic cell division continues: in humans for nine months, in elephants around two years. Next, a foetus takes its first breath. It becomes a baby. An animal with an incredible potential.

The cells continue to divide. The baby grows; it becomes a man. The man marries, perpetuates the cycle. He eats, defecates, sleeps, procreates, works, fights to protect and squirrels his savings, fights to feed his offspring. The man thinks, schemes, suffers, experiences pleasure. He grows old. The cells are programmed to slow down. He deteriorates. He dies. In his life he's done nothing to differentiate him from an animal. Oh, he operated more complex machinery (so does a computer), he learned to add and subtract better than a monkey. He was a smart monkey. A clever ape. He was nice, responsible, loving, he looked after his children. So does a monkey, a fish and a bird. Yet this nice, responsible, loving man, according to Jesus, was never born. Not spiritually. Not into the *real* life.

He remained one of the dead burying the dead.

A human entity that becomes aware of its Higher Self does not die. Gradually it learns to identify with those aspects

---

[26] Individual from Latin *individuus* meaning indivisible, inseparable.

of itself that are immortal. In time, this new entity discards its service accoutrements, the redundant paraphernalia. It frees itself from appurtenances that an animal needs at various stages of its journey towards enlightenment. Still, it is true that the human animal alone seems to manifest such a greater potential.

For good *and* for evil.

For spiritual growth and for material decadence. And for eventual immortality. Barring accidents, the human animal shall find it. It is only a question of time. It could happen in a few billion years. Or tomorrow.

***

961203

The lamps are different,
But the Light is the same.
So many garish lamps in the dying brain's lamp-shop,
Forget about them.
Concentrate on essence, concentrate on Light.
In lucid bliss, calmly smoking off its own holy fire,
The Light streams towards you from all things,
All people, all possible permutations of good, evil, thought, passion.

The lamps are different,
but the light is the same.

Jalal ud-Din Rumi [27]

---

[27] Harvey, Andrew LIGHT UPON LIGHT, Inspirations from RUMI (North Atlantic Books, Berkeley, California 1996) pt. of pg. 14.

7

KNOWINGNESS

The earliest library known to modern man was in Babylon. The collection of clay tablets goes back to the 21st century B.C. Centuries later the Egyptians secreted their knowledge in their temples, hiding it from the people. Their library of Assur-bani-pal[28] was the most noted before the Greek era. We know of the sacred library in Jerusalem's temple. The fame of Alexandria and Pergamum beacons us to this day. The Greek private collections reach back to the 6th century before the present era, and they established their first public library in 330 B.C..

The list of superb modern libraries is endless: the British Museum in London, the Bodleian Library in Oxford, the Bibliothèque Nationale in Paris, the Vatican Library, the Ambrosian in Milan, the Laurentian in Florence, the Lenin in Moscow, the Library of Congress in Washington D.C. where every book copyrighted in the United States must be represented. An enormous emporium of vast human knowledge.

Knowledge, not Knowingness.

The modern man is hungry for facts; enter the encyclopaedias. Collections of data, some odd – some common, famous and infamous, lists upon lists of materials and bibliographies, all neatly stacked up in alphabetical order. Some medieval scholars attempted to make all knowledge available

---

[28] circa 626 B.C. in Nineveh

to the less informed.[29] The modern encyclopaedia tries to do the same.[30] There is no longer any excuse for ignorance. Be it from countless libraries or, more recently, from the computer software, we all can gain access to the intellectual storehouse. To other people's knowledge. We can learn what others thought, did, and aspired to. It is a little like being peeping Toms on a global scale. We can now steal with impunity the efforts of other men and women, appropriate them, make them our own. But none of it is *our* knowledge.

It is not Knowingness.

Knowledge is the heritage of the human race. It is the depository of the efforts of countless people, throughout the ages; the product of sweat and toil, of the incomparable instrument we know as the human mind. The libraries of the world attest to the *intellectual* potential of the human race. In a like fashion, our subconscious is a more surreptitious depository of all events, of all knowledge acquired by an individual human being. There is also, according to Carl Jung, a racial memory that manifests itself as the archetype imprints. Finally, our trillions of cells through their secret encoding system known as the DNA, record, store, and update all information required for our biological survival.

Yet, none of it is Knowingness.

Knowingness always comes *only* from within.

Not from within our physical bodies but from within an intangible source. All who attempted to reach into these esoteric archives, into the origins of all which, in a diluted form, gradually percolates into the domain of public libraries, have not yet found a way to pass on this information to their fellow man in a direct way. This special form of Knowingness is

---

[29] Lexicon technicum (1704), Encyclopaedia Britannica (1771), Encyclopédie (1772) et alii.

[30] As of late 1999 the Encyclopedia Britanica is available on the Internet for free.

knowledge in its purest, undiluted form. It is the raw Intelligence, the Truth beyond all doubt, the indestructible, the immutable, the eternal. We can attempt to tap into this field of untrammelled information. We can also burn our spiritual fingers in the process. It is not a library for the tame, for those who think they know all or even some of the answers. It is particularly not for those who are easily satisfied with other people's knowledge. It is for the brave, the hungry, for the not easily discouraged.

The vast majority of mystics, men or women who established even a momentary contact with this Infinite Source, shall remain unknown. They ventured on their search for knowledge not for the purpose of sharing it with individual men, but to enrich the wholeness of the human fabric. Those few whose motivation was directed to an objective testimony became known as avatars, as saviours, as men so advanced in relation to the humble pilgrim's progress as to be regarded as gods. And gods they were as, ultimately, we all must become.

The mystics found the human language so inadequate that when they wished to communicate with each other they used symbols or secret signs. The transference of this esoteric Knowingness into the exoteric knowledge became the task of the few. Those who had that need deferred to parables, allegories, fables. And thus their teaching became shrouded in myths, while the avatars that strove to liberate us from our ignorance paid a horrendous price. The laws of duality demand an equal force to be raised in opposition. Thus the good, the profound is balanced with the evil, the profane. The Spiritual-intangible became balanced by the religious-material. To all but the few – it still is. Why?

Because it cannot be done.

The Knowingness is available to all. A mystic can point to a direction, but all must take the trip alone.

It is from those avatars that we have learned that our essential being is indestructible. That our true identity is indissoluble from the totality of Life, of Oneness, of the amorphous substance they called Spirit. They all agreed on one point. That unless we look for the divine spark at the very depth of our being we shall certainly not find it anywhere else. Neither in temples, nor in synagogues, nor in churches gilded with statues of saints. It is a lonely journey. But the rewards are, and must remain, beyond words.

***

961220

I knew a man in Christ...
(whether in the body, I cannot tell: God knoweth)
such an one caught up to the third heaven.

II Corinthians 12:2

8

FREEDOM

There are few amongst us who do not recognize freedom as a God's given right. History is abundant with men who preached, beseeched, fought and gave their lives for this most sacred principle of individual freedom. In the Declaration of Independence the delegates to the Congress of the United States speak of all men being endowed by their Creator with certain unalienable rights, among them Liberty.[31]

Liberty ensues from independence, independence from the spirit of liberty.

The Preamble of the American Constitution speaks of securing "the blessings of liberty to ourselves and our posterity". All the articles that follow are illumined by this preamble. The Bill of Rights declared in force December 15, 1791 defines and further protects these rights with particular accent on freedom of the citizenry.

On June 26, 1945, in the city of San Francisco, a text equally authentic in Chinese, English, French, Russian and Spanish reaffirms faith in the "fundamental human rights, in

---

[31] The 2§ of the Declaration of Independence starts with: "We hold these truths to be self-evident, that all men are created equal, that they are endowed by their Creator with certain unalienable Rights, that among these are Life, Liberty and the pursuit of Happiness."

the dignity and worth of the human person, in the equal rights of men and women... " So reads the preamble of the Charter of the United Nations. The first text in the history of the human race addressing all people, men and women – the world over.

How few delegates understood the meaning of such noble precepts.

But we mustn't give up. The charter had been affirmed hardly 50 years ago; a long journey indeed since 1215 when King John of England, at Runnymede, signed the Magna Carta. An early seed for the charters of freedoms to come.

Freedom from whom, from what? Who will take care of us when we're free? Who will tell us what to do, where to work, how to earn our living? Who will tell us what to believe in, what to teach our children, where to send them to school? Who will protect us from the unexpected, the unknown, the unpredictable? What of unemployment? What about our old age? What....???

How dare they give us freedom?

***

Responsibility, no one told us, is the obverse side of the coin of freedom.

781 years lapsed since the singing of the Magna Carta. Are we ready to take on the responsibility of being free? 220 years since the Declaration of Independence. Are we ready for the independence? Are we ready to stand up and walk on our own two feet without the assistance of a king, prince, church, welfare state looking after us? Are we willing to chart our own direction on the turbulent oceans of life and adventure? Or do we demand our illusory rights without paying the dues of birthright.

Freedom without responsibility is anarchy.
Freedom for the select few is oligarchy.

Freedom imposed on children is irresponsibility.
Freedom is a privilege to be earned, not given.

Freedom is an idea.

And ideas are power. Yet to impose one's ideas on others is equivalent to the practice of the blackest Black Magic. We infuse others with concepts that are not yet ready to flourish. We cast pearls before swine;[32] yet swine remain blameless and we are the guilty. Great ideas are sacred and we must cherish that which is holy. Yet we must be so careful. To withhold knowledge from one seeking it is paramount to refusing food to a starving child. The greatest teachers always offered, never imposed their knowledge.

The greater our understanding of freedom, the more responsibility we take on for our brothers. We truly become our brothers' keepers.[33] We begin to perceive that we all are little more than tenants in this world. That we did not create it, that we did little to enhance it, that we hardly deserve to be in it. That up to now we were no more than carefree tots in a magic kindergarten, and that it is time to stand up and look over the edge of our playpen. The world lies outside. A world we have never seen – till now.
It is time, finally, to leave our private Garden of Eden.
We have tasted of the tree of knowledge. We become as gods, knowing good and evil.[34] We learned discrimination. The phase of carefree, irresponsible, wasteful life is over. And as we increase the seeds of our understanding, we begin to take on responsibility for the conditions around us. Our eyes slowly open. We realize that though we cannot be perfect, we can try to do the very best we can. In all walks of

---

[32] Matthew 7:6
[33] Compare Genesis 4:9
[34] Genesis 3:5

life. We make sure that each day, as we retire, we leave the world a slightly better place. Just slightly. Just a little better. Perhaps – a little happier. Perhaps, a little more responsible.

And as we look beyond childhood, we begin to saviour the divine, wondrous, intoxicating attribute of freedom.

***
961217

*We the people of the United Nations
Determined to save succeeding generations
from the scourge of war...
and to reaffirm faith in fundamental human rights,
in the dignity and worth of the human person, in the equal
rights of men and women of nations large and small...
to practice tolerance and live together in peace
with one another as good neighbours...*

THE CHARTER OF THE UNITED NATIONS
signed in the city of San Francisco USA
26th day of June, 1945

9

QUALITY CONTROL

An **American giant,** W. Edwards Deming,[35] suffered from the scourge that affected all the wise men of the past. His own people spurned him. He wasn't the first to be so treated. Luke, the evangelist, said it plainly: "No prophet is accepted in his own country".[36] Then or now. Jesus cried. "O Jerusalem, Jerusalem, thou that killest the prophets, and stonest them which are sent unto thee..."[37] How little has changed in 20 centuries! Oh, we seldom kill our visionaries any more; we do stone them with words though, and with luck, we expel them from our midst.

The unfortunate consequence of this maxim is that by ostracizing the messenger we tend to disregard the message also. It is fortunate, however, that contrary to the prophets of Jerusalem, today's seers can, and do, go somewhere else. The prophets are no longer obliged to teach the hard-necked rabble. The centuries have pushed back, expanded the horizons. No ocean is too great to cross for the message to find fertile ground.

And W. Edwards Deming crossed the Pacific Ocean.

He is best known as the father of Japan's post-second-world-war industrial recovery. And his game plan was really quite simple. Mr. Deming proposed a system which, when

---

[35] Walton, Mary DEMING MANAGEMENT METHOD
[36] Luke 4:24, Matthew 13:57, Mark 6:4
[37] Matthew 23:37

applied to any industrial process, would result in an unparalleled financial success. A tempting offer. Japan listened while America ignored him. Once again the prophet was not accepted in his own country. Who is this Deming to tell us how to improve our quarterly returns, they asked with a smirk on their curling lips. Are we not the greatest world power? Perhaps. But Mr. Deming's teaching not only put Japan at the forefront of the world economy but, in just a few years, it helped the country of the rising sun overtake the U.S. of A. at her own game. And remember, Japan had lost the war!

So what was this Deming secret?

The very same as all the other prophets'.

Mr. Deming advocated quality control. Not so much the quality of the product, as the quality of the *process* which would result in a superior product. It basically meant that a good product is a corollary of a good methodology applied to good, everyday living, ah... pardon, everyday production. He claimed that a good apple usually falls from a good tree. He told the Japanese to plant a good orchard. To never-mind the apples. To use good soil, good fertilizer, to take care of their orchard. Mr. Deming simply stated that if one controls the quality of the process, the end-result would take care of itself.

Take no thought of the morrow: for the morrow shall take thought for the things of itself.[38] It almost sounds as though Mr. Deming had been preaching the gospel! Perhaps the truth doesn't really change. It just finds new applications.

Throughout history this was the teaching of the prophets. Throughout history the prophets had been, and continue to be, misunderstood. People insist on the end-product, on the quarterly returns. On the bottom line. They are result oriented. Yet in terms of a production line, the end-product is as death is to a human being. After all, death is the end-product of our life. And under the circumstances is it any wonder that

---

[38] Matthew 6:34

the prophets had been preoccupied with life? Isn't life a *process* that can be enjoyed enormously, or endured until the final end-product, death, will relieve us from suffering? From Moses to Deming, all the avatars have taught, the few who would listen, the art of living.

They taught us to control the quality of life.

They were never concerned with religions, or with what would happen after our physical death. They never built churches or temples or synagogues. They sensed the omnipresence of the Creative Force. They never found time to be concerned with the ultimate result. It was too far into the uncertain future. They were too busy living each and every day; each successive instant on the endless procession of fragments of eternity.

There is, of course, another explanation for their wisdom.

For anyone who attains the realization of immortality, of being immortal, there can be not such thing as an *end*-product. The great avatars had been so far advanced that they knew, without the slightest doubt, that they were, are, and forever will be, immortal. They knew that a few years sojourn interacting with matter, before discarding their physical envelopes, can be great fun. They also knew that this sojourn is not more than a flicker of an eye in the immensity of existence.

It seems that some of us still don't believe them. In time we shall. Time is what we have so much of. It stretches forever, beyond the furthest rainbow.

***

961216

*"Whoso would be a man
must be a nonconformist.*

*...Nothing is at last sacred but the integrity
of your own mind...
No law can be sacred to me but that
of my nature."*

Ralph Waldo Emerson
1803 – 1882
[Self Reliance]

10

666

There is an old Polish saying: "Work and pray and your hump will grow all by itself"[39]. Admittedly the saying does lose something in the translation, but its intent is to suggest that work and prayer is not all that life is about. In the olden days work had been done manually. The peasants spent long hours doubled-over when seeding, weeding and reaping their crops. After suffering such discomfort from sunrise till sunset for six days in a row, they had been admonished by their priests to bend their backs again and pray to have their sins forgiven. I am at a loss to imagine when did the poor wretches find time or energy to offend their Maker. Anyway, the old saying implies that if you spend your life bent over you will develop a permanent stoop. A posture of penance and defeat.

A good few centuries later, a Polish pope had been elected to the highest office in the Vatican, perhaps the world. The man was young, energetic, with a posture and temperament of an athlete. He loved to ski, swim, sail, and most of all to lose himself among the mountainous trails. No hump would ever bend this man's back. Once an athlete always an athlete.

Or so it seemed.

---

[39] Módl sie i pracuj a garb ci sam wyrosnie.

After some 20 years in office, the Polish pope developed a permanent stoop. Until recently he still took a little time to swim, to take a walk in the piazza. And the rest of the time? He gets up at 5:30 a.m., he prays for four to six (some say eight) hours a day; the rest of the time he works. His schedule is, if anything, longer than that of the olden Polish peasant. He works as long hours as his body, weakened by years of abuse, will allow. An almost permanent grimace of ill-concealed pain contorts his tired features. The once radiant, almost permanent smile is gone. He must bear his cross. He must work and pray. After all, the prosperity of the church still rests on his shoulders.

Are we to follow his example? Does His Holiness serve as a beacon for some 900 million faithful? Did God plan a hump for every one of us – as a reward for a life of service? Or did the Polish peasants know something that the pope lost in his arduous, taxing schedule of ecclesiastical procedures. Is the work-pray ethic that which a Christian must follow? How are we to regard such noble, self-immolating, surely charitable example, in the light of the teachings, which the pope as well as most of us are attempting to follow?

> *"...become as little children".*[40] *"Take no thought for your life, what you shall eat, or... drink; nor yet for your body, what you shall put on.... take therefore no thought of the morrow..."*[41] *"The sabbath was made for man, not man for sabbath."*[42] *"My yoke is easy, and my burden is light."*[43]

---

[40] Matthew 18:3
[41] Matthew 6:25... 6:34
[42] Mark 2:27
[43] Matthew 11:30

And finally:
"...behold, the kingdom of God is within you."[44]

Are these just phrases to please the few, or instructions for *all* of us to follow. Aren't the children supposed to play? ...to be and *feel* innocent, carefree? Aren't we supposed to trust our Father in heaven that He will take care of us as *He* sees fit?

Or are we to stoop under the weight of anxiety.

Are we not to spend the Sabbath rejoicing in the gifts that have been bestowed upon us? Rejoicing in the beauty of nature, the skies, the seas, the mountains, the forests, the birds and the beasts? Is there not enough enchantment in this world for everyone to share and feel grateful – on the Sabbath day?

Or are we to spend the Sabbath stooped on our knees praying for forgiveness.

And should not whatever work we do give us a sense of participating in the creative process of the universe? Are we not created in the image of the Creator Himself? Should we not free ourselves from our yoke by taking it on willingly? With delight?

Or are we to stoop under the burden created by our own will, perhaps our ego.

And finally, are we to labour and suffer throughout our lives, spend years in self-denial, prostrated or on our knees... in order that, one day, perhaps, if all goes right, if we do not commit a sin with the very last breath, if, if, if... If we do not breakdown under this self-imposed, depressing scenario... then we might, just might, "go" to some elusive, enigmatic, incomprehensible heaven? Or should we discover this

---

[44] Luke 17:21

blessed state, this Kingdom of heaven, within our own hearts, within our souls, within our awareness.

If we do, then not even a Polish peasant shall stoop under his burden.

Throughout the Bible the figure '6' occurs many times. Usually, it refers to work. To hard labour. It is the number that precedes the number symbolizing fulfilment. It is the unfinished number, the one that comes immediately before Sabbath. And when repeated thrice, 666 stands for the works of the devil. And what is devil? It is a state of mind. It is that within us which directs our mind to succumb to the illusion of reality, to the world of matter. 666 symbolize a mental condition, which compels us to rely on our *own* power, our *own* intelligence, our *own* devices. It represents those among us who, rather than submitting to the divine spark within us, choose to do the job ourselves. Whatever it is.

Their yoke is heavy indeed.

***

961213

I sought to accomplish whatever was to be accomplished for anyone in such a manner that the advantage attained for anyone would never be secured at the cost of another or others.

R.Buckminster Fuller [45]

---

[45] CRITICAL PATH [St. Marin's Press], *Self-Disciplines of Buckminster Fuller*, pg.125.

11

CELESTIAL & OTHER BODIES

When in February 1987 Sanduleak went supernova and left no remains to tell the tale, the astronomers were stumped. When a star 20 times the size of our sun blows itself into the kingdom come, the heavier elements at its core are supposed to collapse under their own weight and shrink to a much smaller but extremely dense mass called a neutron star. A neutron star with the mass of our sun would be hardly 10 miles across. Now that's denser than my grandmother's Christmas cake – and then some.

When an enigma occurs, the astronomers, the guys who spent all night *watching* the stars, defer to their colleagues, the theoretical physicists. Now these guys don't watch anything much, they just run a hot bath, climb in, and start thinking. Seriously, the theoretical physicists don't observe the world. They observe the observers and whenever the observers get stuck by observing or, as in this case, *not* observing what they were expecting to observe, the theoreticians start theorizing.

"Their ideas derive from an intuition about the way nature behaves on its most fundamental level, the kind of 'feeling', or hunch – almost a personal aesthetic that is every bit as important for a good theorist as the ability to solve equations."[46]

In other words, first you must reach into your intuition, reach into your inner self. Then you order your thoughts into a language you can share with others, work like the devil to translate your ideas into mathematical equations which must fit into the logical processes on which our science is built. Then you ask others to observe if your insight, intuition, your personal aesthetic was right. It's a long process. The world started some 20 billion (give or take a few billion) years ago, and we still have little idea how it works. We must be pretty slow thinkers. According to a cute film called "Defending your life", most of us use between 3% and 5% of our brain. Off hand I'd say that's a slight exaggeration. Most of us haven't started using our brain at all. Except for the cerebellum, to flex our muscles and the medulla oblongata which controls our automatic functions.

So much for the theoreticians. Now a word about the observers.

A lady born in 1913 died recently. Her name was Mary Douglas Nicol, who later married Louis Leakey. She, together with her husband have been observers. Mary had no formal training but she was recognized as "a tremendous archaeologist and paleo-anthropologist all the time."[47] Some reference! All the time! Apparently, she never stopped observing. That, surely, left no time for theorizing. To make sure that we are on the same wavelength, let's define some terms. Archaeologists are people preoccupied with ancient

---

[46] A direct quote from an article MYSTERY OF THE MISSING STAR, by Adam Frank, in the December '96 issue of DISCOVER magazine.

[47] dixit Derek Foe, an Oxford University lecturer in paleolithic archeology.

cultures. They dig and dig until they find something old, and then they do just a little theorizing, but mostly they go right on digging. Paleo-anthropologists we must break down into components. *Paleo-* means ancient; *anthropo-* means man or human, and *logist* is derived from a Greek word meaning: to speak. So Archeo-paleo-anthopo-logist basically refers to a person who talks about what they found while digging. It's not a bad pastime and it certainly sounds important.

But is it?

At one time Mary Leakey, and she was the best, remarked that "All these trees of life with their branches of our ancestors, that's a lot of nonsense." She ought to know. Mrs. Leaky (assisted by her husband) worked in the wilds, enjoying the wonders of nature. It beats soaking in the bathtub! Over the years she unearthed many ancient sculls and other bones. Some of them apish, some proto-human. Yet after a lifetime dedicated exclusively to her passion, she declared that her discovery in 1978 of footprints frozen for 3.5 million years in volcanic ash, which demonstrated that early hominids walked upright, was "the most important find in view of human evolution".[48]

Now I have utmost respect for a woman who spent her entire life doing what she loved doing the most. This very fact is surely her greatest achievement. This and her love of mystery stories and malt whisky. But surely, there are many apes that walk upright *today*, and some of them are not even human.

There is a tremendous gulf between an African jungle and a hot bathtub. But there is one thing which Mrs. Leaky and the theoretical physicists have in common. They had and continue to have a passion for their work. Dr. Hans Bethe, the theoretician, is 90, and he continues teaching at Cornell in

---

[48] She was referring to her discovery at the Laetoli site, south of Olduvai Gorge.

Ithaca. Both scientists reached into the past, but enjoyed it in the present. Perhaps they made a point that time is elastic; or, perhaps unwittingly, that it is less important what you do than how you do it. I doubt that the human race will change its course as a result of either scientist's contribution. Regardless of their findings, the universe shall unfold itself as it should. It did just that, for quite a while, without their help.

Yet, to me, both scientists are philanthropists. Whether they were concerned with the celestial or Paleolithic bodies, by the very love they expressed for their work, they injected a dose of joy into the matrix of the universe. Their contribution shall add sparkle to the texture of the human past, present and future.

Perhaps that is all anyone of us can do.

***

961211

PHILANTHROPY

from Greek *philanthropia*, from *philein*, to love and *anthropos*, man.

[Webster Dictionary]

***

I command you that ye love one another.

[John 15:17]

12

THE DEAD
THE LIVING AND THE DYING

Reaching back for charms and formulas as far into the past as the 16th cent. B.C., the Egyptian Book of the Dead offers sacred instructions on how to cheat death. Somewhat later, the alchemists did more than attempt to turn lead into gold. They attempted to extract the *elixir vitae* from the juices or quintessence of earth itself and direct its recuperative energy into the human body.[49] The Greek mysteries of Hades, the Hebrews' unseen state of Sheol, the Christian hell (Hades resurrected), interspersed with the valley of Hinnom, better known as Gehenna... offer a choice of exits from this earth so unpleasant that one can hardly blame the alchemists for trying to escape the inevitable.

The alternative of heaven, where strumming a harp reputedly provides the only form of entertainment – supposedly driving us into a state of exuberant (or perhaps aberrant) happiness – seemed, if anything, worse.

Thus the search for the elixir of life is as old as the fear of death. It is quite evident that death and not *life* shaped our minds from the ancient times onward; either through many reincarnations or, if you give no credence to this concept, then from early school days. A morbid concept most dear to

---

[49] Gleamed from ISIS UNVEILED by H.P. Blavatsky, Theosophical University Press, California.

the evanescent priesthood, who, generation after generation galvanized fear and foreboding mystery of the future, of the unknown, but mostly just encouraged *fear*. By holding the sword of Damocles over our hardy necks, they successfully managed to control our purses. The Egyptian priests did it, the Greeks found the idea to good to knock, the Roman priesthood added quirks of their own, well... the rest is history.

All because we are afraid to die. One would think that if people were to shed this perennial fear, the priesthood of all ages would go bankrupt overnight. But how? How can we abandon this nagging dread?

There was a time when priesthood not only controlled our minds and emotions but also our bodies. They guarded jealously and protected their medical knowledge (and other sciences) from our uninitiated eyes. Today's expression "knowledge is power" is as old as the ancient sacerdotal power-brokers themselves.[50]

The first snag to hit this system occurred about 4 centuries B.C.. A spoilsport called Hippocrates decided that medical knowledge was to serve people's needs and not be used to subject them into obedience. His famous oaths cooked the goose, or at least some of her golden eggs. For a while physicians had been forbidden to hurt people in order to take their money. But this method got nobody nowhere. The patients continued to suffer and die, and the doctors made less and less money. Something had to be done.

It took quite a while. Gradually, over many generations, the medical profession converted the human species into a race of hypochondriacs. The priest didn't like it but what could they do? After all, it is they who taught people to fear death. Now they had to split the proceeds two ways. It took further generations before the lawyers got onto the bandwagon. I've heard it said that divorce lawyers are the sole beneficiaries of the sacrament of marriage.

But let's get back to the worthy physicians.

Like their priestly predecessors, to this day the illustrious members of the medical profession remain preoccupied with death. Look at the names of various departments in your local hospital. The titles read like a litany of diseases, most of which you had no idea have been already invented. Nowhere does one see a department of Health, of Well Being, or of Cures, or Prevention, or Anticipating or Forestalling or even of Maintenance of our fragile bodies. There isn't even a Department of Prophylactics – though such would, these days, carry some chaste overtones.

Health doesn't pay. After all, if people were healthy the physicians would go broke. This very thought should spur at least some of us to start looking after our bodies better. The doctors won't help us. It is not in their best interest. Yes, there *are* exceptions. There are also saints among the priests, but how many Father Theresas have you met lately? Well?

Anyway, to be quite honest, we just wallow in death. In Verdi's Otello, the demented hero's nasty consort Iago sneers in his superb monologue (roughly translated): "...from the moment of birth I've been condemned to die". We are. In a way. Most of us seem to choose to live in a protracted state of dying. A strange choice.

So much for dying; but what of the dead and the living? We must decide whether we mean the already dead, or the *still* dead, as against the still living, or the *already* alive. It's all very confusing!

Not much has been written about either category. Two thousand years ago a great Teacher claimed that all those who are not yet born of the spirit are still dead. Not *already* dead physically but *still* dead. Spiritually. Little has been said since to challenge this theory. Even less to uphold it. But how exactly are we to be born of this "spirit"? Assuming we are still just a little afraid of death, or even of dying.

Well, it's not all that difficult.

Spirit, according to the same Teacher, is the True reality. He also said that whatever we firmly believe in – *becomes* our reality. It we believe we are immortal, we become immortal. Perhaps not all at once, not overnight, but let's face it, we risk little by trying. We could start by believing we don't have to have a cold. Or a headache. Or that our back doesn't hurt any more. Or that we are smart. Or that whatever or whoever has been smart enough to create such a complex organism, as we all are, is also smart enough to maintain it. If we choose to believe that *firmly*, then gradually our life starts changing. In fact, we are coming awake. Slowly – we come alive. We start living. We begin believing in ourselves. In our potential.

We don't give up on the priests, doctors or even lawyers. Not all at once. But we relegate them to the field of the last resort. We do not run to them the moment we get a running conscience, or nose or bank account. We first try to cope on our own. We start growing up. It's a long journey.

Then, one day, quite suddenly, we start believing in our immortality. It takes a while. For some it could take a few years, for others – perhaps ten or twenty lifetimes. But that's the more reason to start right away. Right now. There is no hurry, of course, but why waste the precious gift of being? We can continue to live in fear; fear for our life, our health, our future. The funny thing is that in time, after we start believing in our own immortality, we no longer care about the future. We are too busy enjoying the present. We forgot how to live in fear.

Why not try it. What do you have to lose?

***

961210

13

BEING AND BECOMING

When I grow up, I shall be such and such. Remember? A doctor, an architect, a scientist, a prime minister, the president of the United States; perhaps a mother of six beautiful children. Ambitions, dreams, plans – the preserve of the young. The age of Becoming. Some of us may have been so busy making plans for the future we had no time to enjoy the day in hand. There are dozens of self-help books on the market, each pontificating that unless we develop a very specific plan and stick to it, come-hell-or-high-water, we shall never amount to anything.

Perhaps. After all, most of us do not appear to amount to much. Perhaps we hadn't made our plans with sufficient diligence. But not Wolf.

Wolf was a pesky child. He would spend hours just playing around. Mostly on the piano. Having fun seemed all he thought about. He would not listen to his father's advice. Nor to anyone else. He was probably the most irresponsible child any parents could imagine. Fun, fun, nothing but fun.

Wolf grew up and... as is to be expected, he continued to ignore the advice of his betters. Having come from a decent family, he had access to very high circles. An illustrious career seemed well within his grasp. But, Wolf was a bit of a wolf. Wine, women and song – not just song but music generally. That's what he concentrated on. And he enjoyed life to the full. Whatever he did – he did his way, paying no heed whatever to the established ways, to proven methods which no doubt would have led him to considerable success on the social ladder. His head seemed filled with a constant stream of ideas to which he succumbed on the spur of the moment. The best one could say about him was that whatever he did, he did all the way. He never postponed anything. He lived in the present. Once an idea struck him, there was no holding him back. And, they said, he was such a gifted young man. Well, the consequences were obvious. He never amounted to anything. Wine, women and song. Lots, lots of song.

It surprised no one when he died young. Very young. And poor. He didn't leave enough money to be buried with any decency or decorum. He was a dismal failure. So said everyone. Just about everyone who knew him.

Was he happy? He always did what gave him the greatest pleasure. Was it worth it? In spite of considerable opportunities and undeniable talent, he failed to rise to top of the society of his day. He was too busy living. Instead of hopping onto the ladder of Becoming, he chose the state of Being. Instead of planning, he acted on impulse. Instead of "working" he did whatever sated his hunger and thirst. He revelled in women. They were such fun. But music was more than that. Music was his passion. And he may have drunk wine to excess. But mostly he emptied the chalice of life itself.

Was he really a failure? Is Becoming a more advanced state of consciousness than Being? How many of us are prepared to give up tomorrow in order to squeeze all out of today? It has been said: "Take therefore no thought for the morrow; for the morrow shall take thought for the things of itself".[51] Wolf didn't and he died young. Is old age a reward for living in a state of becoming? Or is it punishment...?

Imagine giving up most pleasures in life to achieve a great goal and then, on the eve of success, falling under a truck. Seriously, just imagine. Wouldn't you feel like an idiot? I would. People seem preoccupied with the future. They spend fortunes paying prognosticators to find out what is written for them in the stars. Businesses keep on their staff personnel trained in outwitting the future markets of the world. A new term has been coined, not yet in the dictionary: "futurologist". A man who takes your money for telling you what he "thinks" might happen. Or might not.
Usually... it doesn't.
Yet, if you knew the ending of a good suspense movie, would you stay till the end? Or would the rest of the movie seem drab, boring. Do you spend $30 on a good novel and then look up the ending? Would you derive the same pleasure from climbing the mountain if the view on the other side did not offer a promise of discovery? Would any explorer bother to cross the ocean if he already knew what was on the other side? Isn't the unknown always the more fascinating? Do you like *any* surprises?
Or do you find your life an extremely boring experience?

Becoming is fine. We all are in a constant state of becoming. This condition is unavoidable. We live, we develop, we learn, we experience. We apply our senses, we exercise our mind and imagination. But the more we know, the further the horizons seem to recede. The greater the call of the unknown. The more tantalizing the surprises. And as the possibilities multiply, the future, or alternate futures, become even more unknown. And this is the great source of joy for a truly

---

[51] Matthew 6:34

inquisitive mind. The unknown!

Being is rejoicing in today. Becoming will take care of itself. Some have been told by their doctors that they have only a short time to live. They are the lucky ones. Not because they know the future, the doctors are often wrong, but because they are forced to live in the present. To live each and every moment to the full. To rejoice in every second, in every breath. If only we all knew that tomorrow is of no consequence, we too might start living like Wolf. Wolfgang, as he was later known. His middle name was 'Beloved-of-the-Gods". Amadeus. He may not have lived long but he filled his life to the brim. He crammed more exuberance into his 35 years than most do into a 100. He crammed it with song, with wine and with women. With joy.

I know. I heard his music.

***
961202

If music be the food of love, play on;
Give me excess of it, that, surfeiting,
The appetite may sicken, as so to die.

William Shakespeare
[Twelfth-Night]

14

THE UNKNOWN

To boldly go where no man has gone before...

For years we heard captain Kirk recite these words as he embarked on yet another Star Trek. Imagine. After years of service he was free to settle down, to enjoy the fruit of his labours. Surely he deserved it. He'd not only performed above and beyond the call of duty – he risked his life almost on a daily basis. If we didn't know better we would suspect he was a suicidal maniac.

Was he? Were his actions motivated by the dangers inherent in his missions, or was it the desire to *overcome* the dangers, no matter how treacherous, that impelled him on his way. Did he spurn danger out of desire for fame, wealth, position, recognition? Or was he driven by a need to widen his horizons, to gain greater knowledge, to simply go where no man has gone before.

To face the Unknown.

But Cpt. Kirk is a fictional character. No sane man would continue to take such risks if he could, instead, retire in comfort. Or even take a comfortable desk job from which he could drive his comfortable car to a safe, comfortable home, with a crackling fire, a dog at his feet, a glass of cognac in hand. Or perhaps to stretch out on the pristine sand of a Caribbean beach, sip a rum cocktail and...

...and what? And wait for death to release him from subtropical doldrums.

But isn't this the dream of most men you know? Don't most of your friends spend eight, ten, twelve hours a day at their place of work dreaming of becoming a vegetable on a southern beach? Ask them. Ask around how many of them wouldn't, if they only could, throw in the towel, stop the world and get off. They'd call it getting out of the rat race. Millions, veritable millions of dollars, are spent on lottery tickets by people who want to win in order to do just that! And the strangest thing of all is that people who can least afford them buy most tickets. Those in the deepest rut.

But why be a rat in a rut to start with? Why join the race? Why create conditions in which one is forced to spend at least one-third of one's life doing what one hates, or even just doesn't like doing? *WHO forced anyone into such a ridiculous situation?*

I asked around. The answers: I have to support my family. Wife, children, elderly parents. I have to pay off my mortgage, my car, furniture, oversized TV set. I am still paying-off my last vacation. I must put away enough for my pension. I'll need money when I can't work (doing something I hate) any more. Who knows? I need something for a rainy day. Everybody does it – ergo, it must be right. And finally, the worse of all: It's too late now to change.

Sooner or later we all come to a fork in our journey. Which road we choose is by far the most important decision we make in our life:

• Do I choose to be a sheep and follow the established tracks, or
• Shall I listen to my soul and venture into the unknown.

No man nor woman ever avoided this decision. It is as unavoidable as life and death. It is the quintessence of being human. We can follow our instinct or our intuition.

Instinct is derived from the total knowledge accumulated in our genetic makeup from the time our bodies were no more than single cell organism. For countless millions of years, nature, through the process known as natural selection, endowed us with an information storage capacity that enables our bodies to survive. Our body carries this information in very complex molecules called DNA (deoxyribonucleic acid). It is the substance in the chromosomes of the cell nucleus. The individual traits are stored in genes, which transmit the hereditary pattern most apt to help us survive as the human species. They (not the brain) are the memory storage of our biological computers.

The genes, in turn, can be altered. Not just by genetic engineering, but by the activity of enzymes: proteins which act as catalyst for specific biochemical reactions.[52] Our genetic pattern is constantly monitored, adapted and reorganized. A beehive of activity, *all without our conscious knowledge or intervention*. After all, which one of us can add a cubit to our height?[53]

Why don't we play an active part in the survival of our species?

Because *we are not* biological entities that have been programmed, and continue to be reprogrammed, to survive. We are not "our" bodies; we are the tenants of "our" bodies. As tenants we are responsible for not abusing our hosts, for maintaining them in the best order we know how. When we

---

[52] I read somewhere that when we take conscious control of the enzymes in our bodies, we shall control our physical immortality.
[53] Compare Matthew 6:27

err, our host will compensate as best he or she can. It will do so *instinctively*. The cells comprising our host bodies continue to renew themselves on a pattern developed over millions of years. We can learn to *listen* to our hosts and try to cooperate. When we listen to "our" bodies, we act on instinct. We participate in their survival.

So much for the gracious hosts which allow us to use their knowledge acquired over aeons of history. During the last few thousand years we have done little to help our benefactors – we destroyed millions. We pump these bodies full of junk, poisons, smoke and other pollutants. We subject them to an almost constant state of stress. We hardly take them for a walk. We do more for a pet dog! Yet all that is expected of us is not to abuse our hosts' generosity through selfish, thoughtless acts. After all, we are guests!

And what of intuition?

When captain Kirk ventures into the unknown, instinct doesn't help him. Instinct is of little use when it cannot draw on past experience. Instead, the good captain must rely on intuition – a form of insight. It is a knowingness rather than knowledge. Whenever we take our hosts where no man has been before, we, the tenants, must take over. Whether we travel among the stars, cross the Atlantic under sail, partake in any creative act – we face the unknown. Whoever spent hours staring at a blank page, or a mocking glare of computer screen, knows the face of the unknown. The body cannot help us there. We are on our own. Our fingers can write but we must guide them. They offer us their superb agility, result of aeons of evolution, yet they are helpless without us. Without their tenant.

Intuition is to the mind what instinct is to the brain. The brain responds to acquired knowledge, the mind to the infinite field of intelligence that does not yet form part of our experience. Dr. Chopra calls it "the field of infinite possibilities".[54] It is the realm of the bold, the courageous, who do not fear the unknown. It is the playground of those who not only do not spend their lives waiting for retirement, but also refuse to give in when, through unwitting ignorance, all life seems to be squeezed out of our noble hosts. Then, we regard our bodies with gratitude, with kindness and affection. We allow them repose. But rest is not for us. We continue to traverse the unbounded realms in the spaceships of our imagination, on the wings of our immortal soul.

We lay our hosts to rest. We continue forever.

***

961207

---

[54] Dr. Deepak Chopra: AGELESS BODY, TIMELESS MIND. (Harmony Books, division of Crown Publ.)

The important thing is not to stop questioning...
One cannot be but in awe when one contemplates
the mysteries of eternity...
Never lose a holy curiosity.

Albert Einstein

15

I DON'T BELONG

Our civilization seems to suffer from an enormous preoccupation with "evil". In all its forms. The physicians do not talk of health. They talk of diseases. The insurance companies make millions by offering protection from all sorts of bad luck. The politicians keep ramming the national debt right down our throats and pockets. The stockbrokers talk of hedging our bets in order to cover our loses. The priesthood, of all denominations, talk of the countless sins we commit, which will no doubt result in the impending end of the world. Any minute, now.

I am healthy. I carry no life or health insurance. I have no debts – national or otherwise. I do not hedge against, nor do I expect to sustain any loses. I expect the world to continue unfolding itself as it should, without any interference from the malcontent priesthood.

I don't belong.

According to those who wish to treat the Bible as a compendium of historical facts, it's all Adam's fault. He, with a little assistance from the luscious Eve, ate the apple. One lousy apple and – bingo – the world is all to pot. Any god, who would take it out on the present 5.5 billion people, give or take a few far-eastern countries, is not a god I wish to have anything to do with. With or without insurance. For crying out loud! I could understand an evening of debauchery in a greasy-spoon-joint at the local all-night Eden-Eats, or even one oversized and overdressed double-cheese Big-Mac with all the trimmings... but an apple?!

I don't belong.

One allegory leads to another. Once Moses got his message across about the complexities of the creative process, he endeavoured to explain the problem of dualism. Adam is *not* the first monkey that is endowed with human traits. Adam is representative of a soul descending from the "inner" realms, and being encased in a material form. For as long as Adam remains innocent, i.e. for as long as he cannot distinguish between good and evil, rather like little children, his consciousness is unaware of the duality of the reality (world) he entered. We, every one of us, are an Adam, or an Eve, as we enter this world. Our soul, the integral and individualized quantum of the Infinite Reality (referred to by some as God) enters the tiny human form at the moment of birth. Perhaps at the first breath.[55] People often confuse the soul with the body it inhabits. This confusion leads to multiple murders being inflicted by the defenders of life, on those who wish to accord a woman the right to chose what to do with the body she inhabits. The woman's soul, or the one still in abeyance, in waiting, is of no interest to them. They defend an unfinished biological construct. They seem unaware that no one is *for* abortion. Many are for free will of the soul inhabiting the woman's body. The immortal soul decides what to do. Not the body. The body, left to itself, is preoccupied with exactly the same demands as the body of any animal. It wishes to eat, digest, defecate, procreate and sleep. That's what bodies do – they are set on automatic. Strangely enough, particularly at an early age, many animals also like to play. Stranger still, be-

---

[55] In Greek "pneuma" (from *pnein*, to breathe) translates as: breath, spirit or soul. In Christian theology, the Holy Spirit.

cause it is a characteristic of a soul. Children like to play. I am pushing 65. I like to play.

I don't belong.

So what happened to Adam? Since the size of his body is not defined in the Bible, it is not unreasonable to assume that Adam, regardless of his size, was born (created) a baby. God would need less clay, and the job would be faster – the Creator only had one day. The physical size is, however, of no consequence. The Bible deals with the states of consciousness (souls) which inhabit the body, not with the bodies themselves. The soul, therefore, found itself encased in a very uncomfortable enclosure. Just imagine! You're roaming the spiritual realms, and suddenly (time doesn't exist in the spiritual realms), you're trapped inside a little hairless monkey. You scream. You send messages the only way you know how: direct perception. It doesn't work. The mother gets some slight idea and coddles you and you feel an ephemeral whisper of love. It reminds you of home. But it is not the same. "Help!" you repeat this time adding a touch of thoughtwaves you just became aware of. Since you don't yet know human communication, the shout comes out rather like Aooooooow!!! You, the baby, are desperately trying to say: *"I don't belong here!"*

Nor do I.

None of us do.

This is not our home. It is not our domain, our kingdom. It is our school. Temporary. And lessons begin quickly. We watch and observe. Our parents, in fact all the grownups, worry. They are all afraid of just about everything, particularly of tomorrow. They forgot that before they became encased in physical envelopes they roamed the realms where all was Light, all was Good, all was... One. They forgot all that. Instead they divided everything into two components. Into black and white. Up and down. Fat and thin. Good and bad.

Good and... evil? They never stop judging! And they feed us, the newcomers, the very same diet. It tastes like rotten apples. Why can't they understand that the Infinite Reality is One? That there is no good and evil. That God and Good are one and the same. That there is only one, single Source. That we all are indivisible, indestructible, immortal, joyous, wondrous parts of It.

That *that* is where we belong.

***
963011

"...we are strangers on the earth, without permanence, and our days are like a shadow lasting a night, blown away by a wind."

Johathan Eibschutz
1690–1764

16

DUALITY

Every concept inevitably evokes its opposite. The two interact, resulting in a new concept. Or, as Georg Hegel put it, a thesis evokes and interacts with antithesis resulting in synthesis.[56] Thus, black interacting with white results in gray; blue with yellow in green. Every high is balanced by a low. Every darkness can be dispelled with light. Conversely there is no shadow without light. Perhaps the hardest to accept is that there is no good without a smidgen of evil, nor is there evil without an underlying good. There is no synthesis without its structural components. We live in a world of duality. A world of opposites. Yet a world invariably and adamantly tending towards a state of balance.

One could argue that there is little point in expressing one's opinion as it can only result in an "anti-opinion" being promulgated by one's intellectual adversary. The level of intellect is immaterial. Stupid opinions shall be countered by stupid "anti-opinions". Advanced theses shall find advanced antitheses to restore a state of equilibrium in our dualistic world. The Big Bang theory is balanced by the Continuous

---

[56] Georg Wilhelm Friedrich Hegel, 1770-1831, German philosopher. Later the idea of contradictions of opposites had been developed by Marx into dialectical materialism.

Creation theory. This law of duality and balance seems to be as universal as any law of physics which controls our bodies. What goes up, must come down. If you punch someone's chin, the chin will meet your fist with an equal and opposite force (try it on a wall, the owner of the chin might wish to confirm this law on your own chin).

This immutable principle reaches out beyond the physical universe.

It invades with equal force our minds and emotions. He who hates becomes recipient of an equal and opposite hatred. He who kills with the sword seems to die by the sword. This tendency towards the restoration of a state of balance seems unlimited. It permeates our sciences, our behaviour, our emotions, our dialectic knowledge. It punctuates our religions (good and evil), our daily behaviour (tit for tat or an eye for an eye), our relationships (give and take). Snap at your wife and she will snap at you. Unwittingly she will restore a state of balance. It is as though we were puppets unable to snap out of this vicious circle of kill and/or be killed, eat and/or be eaten. The whole human race is going in circles, day after day, year after day, life after life. The Orientals call it the wheel of Awagawan. The circle of reincarnation. For ever?

Is there a way out of this, surely, absurd situation? Must we act like automatons who, in spite of our pompous, arrogant and egocentric assurances, seem nevertheless quite devoid of free will? Is there anything we can do that will *not* result in an equal and opposite reaction?

Yes. We can refuse to play the game of tit for tat. But it's not easy.

In the practice of judo, the act of non-resistance is a way of winning a bout. If your opponent pushes you, you do not push back. Instead you pull, to help him along on his cascading way towards the ground. You do not resist; you bend with the force. That's so only, of course, if you are a good judoka.[57] What happens is that the brutal force destroys *itself* if we refuse to resist it. It is so simple a child can understand it. Children are excellent judokas.

All you must do is *not* resist evil.[58]

It may sound absurd but there is no other way. If you propose any thesis and I do not oppose it, I step beyond the laws of the material universe. The laws of the dualistic universe have no more hold over me. I am in this world but not of this world. I live by my own rules. I am free. I found the truth and it has set me free. Note, I do not have to agree with your thesis, I merely refuse to register my disagreement. I do not impose my opinion on you. I keep my council.

Try it. It is extremely difficult to start with. We are so used to responding automatically with our balancing trick. We automatically assume an adversary position. We have a built-in need to restore the state of equilibrium little knowing that if we step beyond the laws of this universe, the universe will take care of itself. The force, the thesis, the hatred, will dissipate of itself. It has no life of its own. It dies its own puffed-up egotistical death. Its reality was but an illusion. The illusory reality of the physical universe is derived from the interaction of the opposites. The synthesizing process is never-ending, though only for those who wish to take part in it. Mahatma Gandhi did not.[59] Nor did Jesus of Nazareth. There were others.

It has been suggested that God is that which the opposites have in common.

Many great teachings have been deliberately twisted by organized religions who adapted them to suit the requirements of this (the physical) world. Yet the true Reality is *not*

---

[57] Judo evolved from a martial art called ju-jitsu. *Ju* means gentle, *do* means art. Judoka is an exponent of judo.
[58] compare Matthew 5:39
[59] Mohandas Karamchand Gandhi. Mahatma, as he was called, means great-soul.

of this world.[60] Any philosophy, religion or movement, which advocates good *and* evil, as the way of the world, forces its adherents into the dualistic mode. The Truth cannot be divided. It cannot compromise nor be compromised. True monotheism cannot accept the existence of an opposing deity. No matter how inferior. God is One. Even as we are one. Fighting each other, we fight ourselves. It seems silly.

***

961202

> *"To the one Love has instructed,*
> *things that seem opposite reveal their secret affinity and relation.*
> *Show me the evil in this universe in which no good at all is contained,*
> *or the good in which there is not the slightest touch of evil!"*
>
> Jalal-ud-Din Rumi
> [On Good and Evil]
> [61]

---

[60] Compare John 18:36.

[61] Andrew Harvey LIGHT UPON LIGHT, Inspirations from RUMI, [North Atlantic Books, California 1996]

17

CREATIVITY

All knowledge already exists. That which has not yet been materialized exists as a potential state of consciousness. Creativity is limited to bringing out to the conscious awareness that which heretofore has been hidden within.

The awareness of this fact enabled Mozart to write down complete compositions, sonatas, concertos and symphonies, without the need to make a single correction on his manuscripts. He saw or heard them complete, whole. All he had to do was to "bring them out", dispose the notes neatly on music-paper, and hope that performers would do them justice. Great sculptors have been known to say that the work of art is already extant within the stone, within the block of marble. They just had to remove the "unnecessary" pieces of material. The poets hear, or rather feel the poems before they write them down. It is not the process of writing that is creative, it is the art of listening.

Blessed are they who have eyes to see and know how to listen! [62]

It is self-evident that this attitude demands a great deal of humility. We are not really the creators although we partake in a creative act. We are instruments through which cre-

---

[62] compare: "...blessed are your eyes for they see: and your ears, for they hear." Matthew 13:16

ative activity manifests itself in our physical, mental and emotional environments. At best, we are co-creators, though only in a very limited sense. As mentioned before, creation of the world is finished. Complete. All we can hope for is to become aware of its wholeness. To do so we must learn to be silent, then – to see and to listen. To observe.

By the same token, the most to which a writer can aspire is to strike some sympathetic vibrations, some resonant chord within the spiritual memory of the reader. Unless he does, the substance of that which is written simply does not connect with the vibrations of the mind of the recipient. It is not recognized. Perhaps the very same idea, music, work of art, will strike a familiar note at a later date. After all, art, in all its forms, aids the inimitable function of self-discovery.

The discovery of Self, the infinite source *within* us.[63]

I do not refer the Bible to add import to my theses, but rather to point out that these simple truth have been known for thousands of years. Isn't it time to put them into practice? After all, these truths are enunciated for the sole purpose of enriching our lives. Here and now. Emmet Fox wrote years ago that "wealth" is a state of consciousness.[64] The founder of Transcendental Meditation echoed the same sentiment.[65] Deepak Chopra, the physician turned author and lecturer, affirms the same conclusions. Dr. Chopra calls heaven "the field of infinite possibilities". The operative word is *infinite*. We do not have to enhance our life at the expense of another. The source from which wealth comes is unlimited, inexhaustible. There are no rich and poor people. There are only rich

---

[63] compare: Luke 17:21

[64] Nine titles of Emmet Fox books have been published by Harper and Row.

[65] Maharishi Mahesh Yogi (the father of T.M.) when asked from where will the money for a mega-project come, replied: "from wherever it is at present".

and poor states of consciousness. We can be as rich as the ideas that we permit to reach us from within. In this sense, we must be creative.

As the fleeting, spiritual ideas germinate in our unconscious, we must open ourselves to them. We must submit to the thought-streams that flood our awareness. In their own time they gel into fragments of mental images. The catalyst for this process is emotion. It is that which gets us involved, which inspires desire, which instils commitment. When the ideas mature into concrete thought-structures, like Mozart's compositions, they are ready to become manifest in the material universe. That which is beholden in the eye of the artist is whole. To translate this wholeness into material forms, verbal, visual or audible, some of the purity must be sacrificed. Perfection is not a quality of the physical world. The process is often painful, like any birth. This final act is more that of sharing than of creation. That which becomes tangible, detectable to our physical senses, is but a shadow of our thoughts. Remember, the ideas have been complete before we brought them out into the open. A true artist is not really interested in the end product. When a piece of music, a poem, a painting, a sculpture materializes in the physical universe, the authentic artist's work is long finished. He looses interest. History is profuse with masters who delegated this final phase to their pupils.

Spirit is the substance of ideas. Thoughts are the blood of the creative process.

The triad of creativity is comprised of: the creating, the creator, and the creation. The three can be said to correspond to people who are, respectively, interested in ideas, in people and in objects. Generally, the interests are, at least partially, overlapping.

The first group, therefore, are those who are interested

in ideas. Whether the ideas concern spiritual theses, philosophy, the arts, sciences or even business, is of relatively no importance. Every person is endowed with a *different* talent. No two blades of grass are identical, less so the traits of men. Each person must act according to his or her deepest calling. They who succeed are often people who become famous only posthumously. To them the process has been all-important, not the result. In a way, the result has been always there, *in actu*.

The second group of people is preoccupied with the "instrument", i.e. with the messenger. These people are in search of paradigms, or leaders. They still suffer from a great need to follow, to be lead. They find security in belonging to a group. They are still afraid to venture on their own. They build statues to their heroes and they bask in their reflected glory. They are people who love people. Not in the spiritual or unconditional way, but in order to be loved. They desperately wish that they were creative, but humbly assume their self-imposed demotion. They find themselves still unable to assume the full burden of individuality. They also have a great need to help others; they often donate and/or collect vast sums of money to help those who, they believe, had been born unequal.

The third and final stage of creativity corresponds to those whose passion is limited to material, or quasi-material, objects. They are the irrepressible collectors. Their interests include collections of works of art, rare objects, bric-a-brac, souvenirs as well as of titles, medals, recognition and money. All to fill a gnawing hunger, an inner void. They are, nevertheless, the true admires of those who indulge in artistic endeavours. Members of this final group seem quite unable to accept that they too are harbouring unique gifts, hidden talents, which they fail to release. They suffer from a deep, repressed desire to be creative. Paradoxically, they seek escape from having to face the divine spark that lies at the centre of their being.

These, I feel, are the three aspects of creativity. All three thrive within all of us. An accomplished author can suffer from a writer's block. A sculptor can spend days staring at a stone before raising his mallet. Albert Einstein spent many years of his life staring into the stars and still could not "bring out" the Unified Field theory. To tap into the Whole, we must sublimate, often deny, our egos. Sometimes there is a price to pay. Yet regardless of what some will say, it is always an individual choice.

"Ye are gods" proclaim the ancient scriptures.[66] We all truly are. Co-creators. Gods-in-waiting. All we must do is to accept the challenge. All of us.

***

961219

---

[66] John 10:34, Psalms 82:6

*Anyone who has never made a mistake
has never tried anything new.*

Albert Einstein

18

OLD AGE
?

No. It is not my intention to share with you my thoughts about old age. Quite the contrary. I want to share with you that which you already know, but, perhaps, are too set in your ways to admit to yourself. I want to discuss the concept of New Age. Why? Because Old Age is a state of mind. And it's... old. Stale. Atrophied. And New Age is also a state of mind: An Eternal Beginning.

Most orthodox "believers" hate the idea of New Age. Most people, contrary to their often-strenuous assertions, experience an atavistic fear of all things new. The thought of the unfamiliar fills them with paralyzing fear. A new dress, skirt, or a pair of shoes is their idea of new horizons. They seem to have lost all curiosity. Well, they needn't worry. They are firmly set in the Old Age. And until they overcome their fear they shall tread water – a concept as close to the ecclesiastical concept of eternal hell as I dare to venture. Truly, Old Age is a state of mind.

Paul (the apostle) said that he died daily, thereby assuring the freshness or newness of his tomorrows.[67] By Paul's standards, anyone who is afraid of tomorrow, quite simply, is

---

[67] 1 Corinthians 15:31

not a Christian. Paul's own teacher *in absencia*[68] tells us not to worry about tomorrow.[69] In fact we are told not to be afraid. Not even of death. "Though I walk in the valley of the shadow of death, I will fear no evil", says David.[70] We are also told that we are *never* alone.[71] So why are so many people so fearful of those two innocent words? Do they have any idea what the New Age implies?

To fundamentalists, New Age is a heresy devised by devil to destroy the established churches. They think of New Age adherents rather as John the Baptist thought of Pharisees[72], an opinion shared later by his Master. But in fact, there is no one person who brought about the concept of New Age. Rather it is a reawakening to the immutable, indestructible truths of yore, which appear to have been diluted by ages of neglect. Anyone who takes the trouble to delve deeper into the more serious consequences of this new perception will find nothing there which had not been written in the past, in the ancient philosophies of India, Egypt or Greece, and most of all, in the Bible. Of course, this fact is not immediately apparent. Only to those who seek, who knock... only to them this truth is made available.

A single word which gives a taste of New Age is Renaissance. A Rebirth. It implies what we should do, and Paul did, had done, every morning. A concomitant of a new birth is an acceptance off all things new.[73] New Age demands of its adherents to accept whatever the Spirit commands them,

---

[68] Paul never met his mentor, Jesus of Nazareth. Born at the beginning of the 1st cent., a Roman citizen, he was only converted at abt. 35. By then Jesus had been crucified.
[69] Matthew 6:34
[70] Psalm 23:4
[71] ibid.
[72] Matthew 3:7, 23:13 et al.
[73] Revelation 21:5

on the spur of the moment. It also defines a certain Coming of Age. "When I was a child, I spoke like a child, I understood as a child, I reasoned as a child" says Paul, but now "when I became a man, I put away childish things".[74] And so it is with the New-Agers. They put away childish things. When Paul, travelling the Greek islands, wanted to know what to do, how to act, what to say, he could not run the Master. The Master was dead. Nor could he refer to the disciples who heard all the Teaching first hand; they were far away, in Palestine. Nor could he ask a bishop or a priest. There were none. The sacerdotal structure had not yet been created. Paul was forced to do what every aspirant of the New Age attempts to do: to reach deep within his or her consciousness and find out what has always been there. The fount of Truth. The divine spark.

The Higher Self.

The Soul.

Somewhere, during the last 2000 years, this method had been lost. Slowly at first, then ever faster, the vainglory of power has displaced the mainstay instructions left to us: look within,[75] and love one another.[76] That's all. That is the sum total of the original instructions describing the social, public, private, international, worldly relations. *Love one another.* And contrary to all that are ignorant of the tsunami of the New Age, these instructions are the cornerstones on which this present age is being built. We no longer ask opinionated strangers, sacerdotal keepers of the Old Age, how we should relate to each other. We do not ask how to love, how to treat our neighbour. The Truth is within us. We do not attempt to put new wine into old bottles.[77] We empty our consciousness

---

[74] 1 Corinthians 13:11
[75] Matthew 17:21, Romans 14:17
[76] John 15:12
[77] Matthew 9:17

of all appurtenances, of all the dross accumulated by listening to our (and other's) egos, and we open our eyes and ears to the single source which is within everyone who cares to make an effort to find it. Only then can we be filled with the intoxicating nectar of Truth.

Sadly, the New Age game is not for everyone. Only the grownups can play. Only those willing to take full, complete, responsibility for every word they utter, every act they perform, every emotion they allow to emanate from their hearts. We, who wish to take part, shall all make mistakes. Lots of them. But we shall blame no one for our errors. Not the prime minister nor his government; not the system nor the society; not any general, superior, teacher, priest or rabbi; not our mother nor father, nor our neighbour nor friend; neither fate nor luck nor....

Neither anyone nor anything.

We have come of age. A New Age. We, and we alone, shall take the full credit and the full blame.

Like the great Masters of the past we shall place our tentative feet on the new paths. For most of us it will be a long journey. Yet I am as sure as I am of my immortal soul, that one day we too shall become masters. Perhaps not as great as some in the past, but we shall become the focal points at which the Universal shall find Its expression through the particular. The Father and the sons shall become One.

And in an endless procession of the Zodiac, that day will mark yet another New Age. Like tomorrow. And every morning. And, as in any New Age, the only truly new thing about it shall be – you. Your state of consciousness.

And mine, I hope.

***

970101

19

SELF

Life is a search for happiness. We spend lifetimes chasing this elusive rainbow. Paradoxically, the proponents of various religions unanimously issue a guarantee on achieving such a blessed state. After death, of course. In heaven. After they liberate us from our worldly ties. Midas, like his sacerdotal successors, attempted to find happiness this side of the great divide. Alas, to no avail. And yet...

And yet among all the false prophets there was one Man who promised happiness here and now. Happiness for the *living*. He also said that the truth will set us free. And that the truth, and the knowledge, and even happiness, all lay within us.

Within us? Here and now?

We don't have to die to be happy?

The modern gurus manage to generate considerable confusion in this area. Some admonish us to identify with our Higher Self, never explaining what is this enigmatic entity. Others talk of sanctifying our lower self until it is "saved". The first group is predominant among the adherents of eastern philosophies; the second finds its base in the western religious systems, particularly Christianity. Yet to a student of both sources, ranging from the Sanskrit Vedas to the Bible, neither of the assertions seems accurate. Since all sources, however, assure us that the Truth is one, in the interests of brevity, I shall confine myself to the western and biblical influences and terminology.[78]

Why the dichotomy between the Higher and lower selves?

The reason lies in oversimplification of the thesis. A closer study indicates that there are not two but three aspects to the human condition. The first two are subjects of scientific study and can be defined in psychoanalytical terms as the ego and the id,[79] or the conscious and the subconscious selves.[80] The Bible identifies these by the first two syllables of the name Israel, though in reverse order. *Is* represents the passive or the subconscious, while *Ra*, the active or conscious aspect.[81] As already reviewed in a number of essays, *Is* also symbolizes the animal soul *(nephesh)*, or the sum-total of physical or material acquired knowledge. The modern science could endow the DNA with the repository of this trait.

Next comes the most histrionic jump in our spiritual evolution. The knowledge lies dormant within our unconscious, ever ready to be brought into conscious awareness. This phase in our *spiritual* evolution is described in the Bible in the parable of Jacob being renamed Israel. Jacob sym-

---

[78] H.P Blavatsky points out in ISIS UNVEILED that the Vedas which antedate the Jewish Bible by many ages have been the source of considerable "borrowing" by later scriptures.

[79] MAN AND HIS SYMBOLS, Carl G. Jung, (Dell Publ. Co., Inc.)

[80] Margaret J.Black in FREUD AND BEYOND (Harper Collins publ.) writes: The id is a "cauldron full of seething excitations" of raw, unstructured, impulsive energies: the ego is a collection of regulatory functions that keep the impulses of the id under control; the superego is a set of moral values and self-critical attitudes, largely organized around internalized parental imagoes.

[81] Is, or Isis, is the Egyptian nature goddess; Ra, the Egyptian sungod; It is fascinating to note that Isis was symbolized by a cow, suggesting Hindu influences.

bolizes a soul aware of its spiritual nature, but not yet of its divine origin. The name Israel represents a soul that embarks on a *conscious* search for the divine spark within.

A conscious search for Higher Self.

In the Bible, this enigmatic concept is represented by the last syllable of the name Is-ra-el. *El* symbolizes the personalized spiritual nature of man. This highest aspect of man corresponds, in general terms, to the superego, which refers to that part of the psyche that controls at the unconscious level the impulses of the id.[82] In psychological terms the awareness of *El* is a milestone in the development of our psyche. Once we accept the concept of our divine origin, we can no longer refute responsibility for our actions. We can no longer blame countless organizations, systems or individuals for our misfortunes. Not even our destiny reputedly etched in the stars. To paraphrase the words of the psalmist, we are gods.[83] Or at least we have taken the first step towards becoming one with the divinity manifesting Itself through us.

And so, within a mere few thousand years since the concept of Is-ra-el was proposed, man came up with a modern echo: the id-ego-superego concept. How time flies when you're having fun!

But it's not all fun and games. While, say, 20 years of schooling and midnight oil might make you a reasonably competent physician, there are no such guaranties on the spiritual journey. Many charlatans will tell us that if we are good, we shall be saved. Not so! When we are saved, we shall be good. Not before. "There is none good but one, that is God" says the Rabbi.[84] So what are we to do?

We become as scouts – prepared. We learn to live in

---

[82] WEBSTER DICTIONARY, 2nd ed. (Collins World)
[83] Psalm 82:6: I have said, Ye are gods; and all of you are children of the most High.
[84] Matthew 19:17

constant expectation. We try to emulate the object of our contemplation. Ten years of daily training will not guarantee us an Olympic medal. We'd better make sure that we really enjoy the exercise!

While spiritual consciousness is above all concepts of logic or mental gymnastics, the journey is not without its rewards. We might not become spiritual giants overnight, but the potential is there, and we begin to register perceptible changes. Hardly knowing why, we become more contented, serene. We do not seem to worry as much. We are even filled with a strange feeling of being protected. We develop a consciousness of abundance. We are glad to be alive.

And this is only the beginning.

The journey towards a greater awareness of our Higher Self is characterized by progressively identifying with the Whole at the expense of the particular. The illusory separation between 'you' and 'I' loses its intensity. As the ego weakens so does the polarization, so does, what the Orientals call, *maya*. Our reality becomes homogeneous. We discover the singularity of the source, of our origin. And another strange thing happens. We begin to regard our physical body as no more than a shadow cast by the soul. Our priorities change.

***

It is not an easy journey.

The tepid, the half hearted are the greatest losers. They lose the illusion of physical reality and gain nothing in exchange. They are the lost, the undecided, uncommitted. They are straddling the fence. They try to serve two masters. It cannot be done.[85]

The journey of Self-discovery is a journey of love. As suggested before, if we embark on this journey, we must be

---

[85] Matthew 6:24

sure we enjoy it. If we don't, the chances are we are going the wrong way. What joy the biblical model brings is amply illustrated in the Psalms. As for rewards, well, let me count the ways...

We are told to ask so that our joy may be full.[86] Full, here and now. Nobody ever made me a better offer.

***
970102

*"It is not in our stars but in ourselves
that we are underlings"*

Shakespeare
[Julius Caesar]

---

[86] John 16:24

*"In order to be an immaculate member of a flock of sheep,
one must above all be a sheep oneself."*

Albert Einstein

20

A HORSE OF A DIFFERENT COLOUR

In our discussion about SELF, we are reminded that, in psychoanalytical terms, the human entity is defined as:– the ego, the id and the super-ego. Biblically speaking, this triad corresponds to Ra, Is and El, as proposed in the name Is-ra-el, which symbolizes our conscious, subconscious and the Higher Self. The triad defines what or who we are. For our behaviour pattern we must search further.

The astrologers will tell us that our comportment is predetermined by or in the stars. If you are born a Fish you die a fish. Presumably you're all wet. A Scorpio pinches, a Taurus will gore, a Libra presumably liberates, while a Leo will claim a lion's share. Seriously though, we supposedly tread water in one of the 12 cycles of the Zodiac. Whatever our stars decide we're stuck with. Or, at the very least, we are stuck with an overpowering predisposition towards manifesting certain traits. We are set on automatic.

Carol S. Pearson reduces the number of ruts to six.[87] She calls them archetypes and, broadly, elaborates on Carl Jung's concepts.[88] She calls them "deep and abiding patterns in the human psyche that remain powerful and present over time". Sounds to me that we are stuck again, even if we are allowed to change our ruts from time to time. Goody! But I'm not impressed.

The psychiatrists dissatisfied with such a limited mode of expression offer us the syndrome of multiple personalities, the DPM. Apparently, this syndrome likens our "selves" to a ship full of people with no one at the helm. I understand that "one psychiatrist convinced a patient she had 120 personalities (including a duck), and billed her (no pun intended) insurance company for group therapy.[89] Our various traits surface periodically, at random, stimulated by desire to be heard, recognized, or just appreciated. While this syndrome is classed as neurotic, sometimes psychotic, I have experienced it on many occasions. There are times when I feel like Lizzie Bodren, other times, like Lucrezia Borgia; and I *know* I am always innocent of whatever I might be accused![90]

So what, you might well ask, has all this to do with horses?

Plenty.

Many years ago, St. John the Divine received a Revela-

---

[87] THE HERO WITHIN by Carol S. Pearson (Ph.D.) (Harper San Francisco). The 6 archetypes proposed are the Innocent, Orphan, Wanderer, Warrior, Martyr and Magician.

[88] MAN AND HIS SYMBOLS by Carl G. Jung (Dell Publ. Co.) Jung is credited in originating the concept of archetypes as well as on elaborating the notions of id and superego.

[89] Added on 97.11.05, from SATURDAY NIGHT, September 1997, "Sybil minds" by Carol Milstone.

[90] Contrary to popular belief, Lizzie Borden's trial ended with a verdict of not guilty, while Lucrezia Borgia won esteem through her kindness and piety, despite unfounded rumors of her psychotic inclinations.

tion. In it, he had been assured that rather than there being many individuals in a single ship, there is but one individual in many ships. Only, being a landlubber individual, John preferred horses to ships.

The Revelation, known to some as the Apocalypse, postulated that while accepting the concept of the triad presented above, only the conscious, or the ego, is the skipper, sorry, the rider of the various horses.[91] And the stallions, being horses of a different colour, symbolize our principal characteristics, call them archetypes if you must, which we *choose* to ride. In other words, John proposes that we are entities endowed with at least a degree of free will. Of course there are influences, including the stars, the weather, the number of flue viruses floating about, or what we had for dinner last night. Everything is interwoven, everything is relative, and everything affects us. We, however, decide *how* we are going to be affected by the surrounding universe. We have to. In a way (subject to be discussed later), we created the universe we live in.

According to John, we react to external (as well as internal) stimuli in four principal ways. We can treat them as exclusively physical phenomena. When we do that, we ride a pale horse. We are told that this is a very abortive *modus operandi*. The Bible is a textbook of *spiritual* knowledge. Anything remotely physical is used only as an illustration, usually, with rather negative connotations. A person identifying (exclusively) with his or her physical body, i.e. riding a pale horse is compared to Death itself and his or her state of mind – to Hell. Elsewhere in the Bible people who are not spiritually awakened are compared to the dead. The pale horse is a biblical oxymoron.

Unfortunately the red horse is not much better. It symbolizes our emotional nature. This facet of our personality has great power. Power to kill, to destroy, and particularly, to re-

---

[91] Revelation 6:2 at al.

move peace. Not a single war was ever fought on a rational basis. War is an emotional response to an irrational problem. Only mastering this steed can restore peace in our lives.

Next comes the black horse. It, in turn, symbolizes our mental body. I must stress again that we are always the same riders but we act and react in different ways. The mental or intellectual way is cold and calculating. It is devoid of feeling. It counts, judges and carries out the sentence. It is empty, hollow inside. I feel shivers just thinking about it.

And then there is the white horse. He who rides this stallion is a winner. The white horse goes "forth conquering, and to conquer". The rider wears a crown. His hand holds a bow with which he can reach afar, control his domain.

The white horse symbolizes our spiritual nature.

The same rider, the same ego, the same self, riding any or all of the four horses. But unless you are a circus performer, you'll find it next to impossible to ride more than one steed at a time. We make a conscious selection of the horse we wish to ride, and we bear the consequences. And by the way, we bear the consequences regardless how cold and unfeeling or irrational, emotional or instinctive behaviour we exhibit. The cosmic law states that ignorance of law is no excuse for breaking it. This immutable ordinance is known as the law of Karma. Essentially, it is the law of cause and effect. Every cause has its effect. What goes up must come down; as you sow so you shall reap; as you do unto others... etc.; quite simple, really.

There is another principle that is less overt in the Bible.

Apparently, when we learn to ride the white horse, all other horses come in line. Therefore, rather than destroying the characteristics of our lower nature, we bring them all under the control of the rider. In biblical language, we sanctify them. But this only happens when we mount the white horse. The other horses will not follow any other.

Finally, a word about the rider. Consciousness, or the sentient principle, is a quality of the soul. It functions at all times, regardless of the condition displayed by our physical body. The rider represents our consciousness. Only by fully grasping the quality of our nature, can we lift ourselves above the animal state of automatically or instinctively responding to external stimuli. The spiritual nature of man, the soul, is also the causative principle. In all other roles we play, all other horses we ride, we merely react.

We are all furnished with a stable of personal, private, magnificent horses. Physical, emotional, mental and spiritual steeds. Horses of a different colour. When saddling, let us be sure we're not colour-blind.

Happy riding.

***

970108

*"I want to know how God created this world.
I am not interested in this or that phenomenon,
in the spectrum of this or that element.
I want to know His thoughts;
the rest are details."*

                    Albert Einstein
                    1879 – 1955

21

CYCLES

Told that one is walking in circles would be considered an insult. Or, at the very least, it would go a long way to suggest a limited mental capacity. I am in great danger of loosing a considerable segment of my none-too-numerous readers by suggesting that a much more numerous segment of the human race is, in fact, walking in circles. In order to retain at least some of my public, I took the liberty of substituting *cycles* for circles.

Voilá! Much more palatable.

Deep down we all know that the difference between the two is marginal. At best, a cycle offers limited hope of a gradual rise along the track left by our efforts. The cycle while inscribing the very same 360° sounds better. More scientific.

Feel better now? Do you?

I don't.

The cycles can be expanding, drawing ever-larger circles, broadening forever-receding horizons. The cycles can also be converging on a diminishing radius, in ever decreasing er... circles, until we reach a vegetative state of standing still.

Yet, strangely enough, that is not the worst. Our civilization manages to actually regress our ethical development. The more laws we feel obliged to enact the more we affirm our reversal towards a primitive existence. Hammurabi may have been proud of his code, but to me it was the beginning of the end.[92] Surely "advanced" members of the human race are guided by higher laws, by inherent, immutable ethic, not by a set of presumptuous rules created by over-puffed politicians, for their own benefit, i.e. to protect their ill-begotten loot. Look at the taxation laws. Who benefits more from them than the politicians? Who gets life, inflation-augmented pensions from public coffers? Who never produced *anything* worthwhile (in office) while penalizing all that do? Are there exceptions? Surely. Do you know any?

Let's face it, Hammurabi was a brilliant politician.

Let's get back to cycles. They come in various sizes. The largest or longest known to man are the cycles of the Zodiac. The Procession of the Equinoxes advances in cycles of a little over 2000 years each. And each of the 12 signs of the Zodiac represents a new trait of character which we are to conquer, or at least improve on. Good luck. It would help if we all knew what trait we are supposed to work on. Yet, the #1 best seller of all time is replete with references to the Zodiac! The complete Zodiac may seem the longest cycle, some 25,000 years, but it only seems long. The most persistent cycle is the wheel of Awagawan. It is a name given by the Orientals to the cycle of reincarnation. Many avatars left instructions on how to step out of this vicious cycle, but to no avail. Why listen when we're having fun?

We are having fun, aren't we?

Then we have the cycles known as biorhythms.[93] Four pages of bibliography back up a book bearing the cycles' name. It looks impressive, but the cycles are also set on

---

[92] Hammurabi (1792-1750 B.C.), king of Babylonia.
[93] Gittelsom, Bernard BIORHYTHM (Warner 1980)

automatic. Like the Zodiac, like almost everything. If we don't live consciously then we are subject to all the immutable laws of these cycles. Are you? The whole of nature is set on automatic. Many of us are proud to be part of nature. We just love mother earth. Others think it's all just an illusion. Maya.

Take your pick.

And then there are the socio-political cycles. They also seem to be set on automatic, or at least, run by automatons. That's a polite word for robots or people not yet fully alive. The living dead. This cycle runs as follows. The craftier individuals make money at the expense of the dumber elements. This usurped wealth gives them power. They exercise it indiscriminately until they can't cope with the rebels any more. They then contact their like-minded scoundrels and form oligarchies. This works for a while but... alas, you can't fool all the people all the time. The rebels rise their ugly heads and they cut off the heads of the scoundrels. Or maybe they're just tired of eating cake. Anyway, this is called a revolution. Fairly recently the French and the Russians were good examples of such a turn of events. And Latin America is second to none in applying this cycle. Anyway, after the rebels win, they form their own oligarchy, which in time gets clobbered by the masses. *L'histoire se repete.* That's why is called circles. Ah, I mean cycles...

In the West we are approaching the end of another cycle. A two-class society where the growing chasm between the few haves and the many have-nots is a sure sign leading to another revolution.[94] Don't believe me? Study your history. The cycle never failed. Never. After all, it's set on automatic.

---

[94] In Norway the CEO is earning 2-3 times the workers salary. In the U.S. of A. the CEO have scored up to $46 million in one year. That's even more than an illiterate baseball player. [ad int., by February 2001: The CE0s' incomes, including bonuses and stock options exceeded $125,000,000 in one year]

For the life of me, I cannot understand why some people think that there is a Deity up there, somewhere, which will suspend the incredibly complex system IT has devised to run this incredibly complex universe, with its incredibly complex interrelationships, and answer their puny prayers which might contravene the automatic setting. Would God create laws in order to ignore them? Would that be smart? What do you think?

Is there a way to step off this mad merry-go-round going absolutely nowhere? Must we continue to crawl in circles?

Well, what do you think?

***

970104

"In order to be an immaculate member of a flock of sheep, one must above all be a sheep oneself."

Albert Einstein

22

PLEASURE

Hedonism, narcissism, egoism, onanism, masochism or fetishism – individually, or nationalism, socialism, fascism, chauvinism, and what-have-you-ism – jointly.[95] The lists are endless. The first group tends towards the orgasmic, the second – orgiastic. Not much to choose between them. No matter. There follow the delights of the seven deadly sins (pride, covetousness, lust, anger, gluttony, envy, and sloth). Of these I find lust and gluttony most pleasurable while impersonating a three-toed sloth sounds just right after a hard days work. All the above may or may not be accompanied by booze and tobacco as well as other softer or harder drugs, overindulgence of any sort, in any area, and a vast array of self-gratifications of any and every kind. Surely, all the above have been devised to give us sensory pleasure or, at the very least, to stimulate our pleasure centres. Why on earth would people indulge in them if it weren't so? And we certainly do indulge in them. Don't we?

Shall I draw you a picture... or would that be overindulgence on my part?

Loving life is what pleasure is all about. Isn't it?

---

[95] Those who equate onanism with masturbation, I refer to Onan in Genesis 38:9 to see if they continue to do so. The biblical reference notwithstanding, I include it with all other abortive excesses to which people subject their mind and body.

So why are so many religions bent on restraining our boisterous natures? Why have they invented the word "sin", and keep cramming it down our throats? Don't they know that the word sin (in the New Testament) is translated from the Greek word for *hamartia* or *hamartano* which originated from the sport of archery? That its literal meaning is: "missing the mark"? That's right. Not going to hell, not begging for forgiveness, not beseeching absolution – but MISSING THE MARK.

What mark? Most of us don't even do archery.

True, but we do miss the mark.

Loving one's neighbour as oneself does not necessarily refer to our neighbour's wife. Enjoying food does not necessarily lead to obesity. Taking a glass of wine does not imply getting stoned. Smoking sausages over a campfire does not imply, as president Clinton will attest, that we're inhaling. But even a puff or two of tobacco wouldn't hurt us. Sporadic fumigation with carbon monoxide would not enhance our mental dexterity, but would not necessarily result in cancer either. Know anyone who smokes two puffs a day for any length of time? I tried it once. I lasted a whole week – before reverting to a pack a day.[96]

Get the drift?

It's not having fun that misses the mark; it is having it to such excess that it *destroys* our pleasure. When I refuse yet another drink it's not because it is sinful to drink. I refuse it because drinking gives me pleasure. A pleasure I might have to give up if I became an alcoholic. We risk loosing our pleasure by over-indulgence. Maybe Buddha was right. Imagine... Siddhartha Gautama lived in the 5th century BC.[97] What made those ancients so smart? Anyway, we could try

---

[96] Don't worry. I stopped insulting my intelligence 15 years ago.

[97] Siddhartha Gautama c.563-483 B.C. who became Buddha (Sanskrit for "the enlightened one"), was the son of a ruler, became an ascetic, before finding the Middle Path.

his "middle path".

But how about getting pleasure at other peoples' expense. How about acting like the politicians? Maybe they do want *us* to tax *them* silly, and then draw pensions as high as theirs at *their* expense? Maybe we too can be paid exorbitant salaries for mismanaging billions of other people's hard earned dollars. Maybe running up a national debt is fun! I heard it said that only a saint would agree to become a president of the United States – but only a fool would volunteer. And just who elects the president? George Jean Nathan, a critic, once said that bad officials are elected by good citizens who do not vote.

Stop blushing. I know how you feel!

So can we have any fun?

Not according to most churches which insist that we are all depraved sinners. Just listen to Billy Graham. Maybe he forgot (not being a catholic) that even the original sin had been invented by St. Augustine in 4th century AD. The concept does not exist in the Christian Bible nor in the Jewish Torah. And so says Matthew Fox, a catholic priest!

If, however, we stop listening to those who benefit from calling us sinners and listen to the one who gave us the golden rule, we can have just about all the fun we want. All we must remember is to do unto others as we would have them do unto us. Personally, I feel that leaves me an awful lot of elbowroom.

But what about the politicians? It is fair...?

Assuming our eventual return to this planet to enjoy the consequences of our choices of pleasures on our previous visit, I wouldn't trade their pensions for a good night's sleep (I assume *they* can still sleep). We might consider selecting the menu of our self-and-or-mutual-gratification very carefully. Because one thing is as sure as tomorrow's taxes. We shall return. Some self-appointed experts will tell you that this, present "life", this incarnation, is the only one you'll ever have. Not a bad idea if it spurs you towards a better selection. Unfortunately these same experts who encourage you to collect your rewards in your afterlife, fail to specify where and how exactly will this afterlife unfold itself. In the meantime, you transferred all your earthly possessions to these very same advocates who prefer to enjoy the goodies while they can. Right now!

As for myself, until these same experts give me half-decent directions on the whereabouts of my future existence, I will assume, safely I feel, that if my "afterlife" will not be on earth, then it will be in a purgatory (even if it does sound like a clinic for people suffering from constipation). And what better place than earth for a ready-made purgatory. This is where we learn pretty fast how to avoid missing the mark. And how to indulge in pleasure. Safely. At least most of us learn. Perhaps for the politicians there is another place. I wouldn't know.

So Hedonism isn't so bad after all.

With the menu ranging from the sensual titillation of the Cyrenaics to the rationally aesthetic desires of Epicureans, we all search for pleasure. If heaven is to be the fulfilment of our ultimate pleasures, than isn't missing pleasure a sin? Aren't we supposed to strive towards heaven? Perhaps all we really have to learn is to share our pleasures with others. Wouldn't it be fun if love gave us pleasure? If we got a kick out of loving our neighbour. Or even his wife. Or her husband. Or both of them. Platonically, of course. Or better still – loving the whole neighbourhood. Or our whole village. Or town.

Or the world.

***

970105

23

PRAYERS

Prayer is as old as man's insecurity. Plato advised us to remain silent in the presence of gods until they remove the cloud from our eyes and enable us to see by the light that issues from within. Appolonius held his "conversations" with God in isolation.[98] Plotinus recommended solitude for prayer.[99] Jesus suggested that when we pray, we should enter into our closet, shut the door, and pray to our Father in secret.[100] For some reasons, the Christians prefer to build imposing temples, ignoring the advice.

They are not alone.

All religions known to me like the idea of gathering their sheep under one roof. Perhaps it's easier to keep a watchful eye on them, when herded together. But there may have been other reasons. Some prayers were kept secret from strangers. Apparently not only some gods are jealous, but some faithful are jealous of their gods. "The most sacred names of the gods, the prayers by which their favour could be gained, were kept secret. No religion was more exclusive than that of the Brahmans", claims Blavatsky.[101] Epicurus

---

[98] Appolonius of Rhodes, (3rd.cent.B.C.) poet, author of Argonautica
[99] Founder of neoplatonism (c.205-270)
[100] Matthew 6:6
[101] ISIS UNVEILED, H.P.Blavatsky, (Theosophical University Press), vol.1. pg. 581.

(341–270 BC) put it blandly or perhaps bluntly: "The gods exist, but they are not what the rabble suppose them to be".[102]

In spite of all of the above, when stirred with some tempting desire or threatened by an impending danger, I used to resort to prayer. I don't do that any more. I don't have to. I've learned that there is a tremendous misunderstanding, which hoodwinked the people of the world for thousands of years. Some errant tourist skimming the outskirts of the higher realms got the wrong brochure and we've been bamboozled ever since. And that is why, most of us, still pray. We ask, beg, supplicate, fast, eat or abstain from certain foods, practice austerities. We try to meditate and/or contemplate to procure desired effects. Some of us dance, sing, and perform religious skits. We produce works of art and offer them to our gods. But most of us, most of the time, just beg.[103] We desire health, wealth, happiness, security, love (sex), affection, company, talents, enlightenment – anything that will enhance our lives.

The question is why should we pray at all?

Aren't we told that the Father knows what's best for us? After all, the very hair on our heads are numbered.[104] And even during all the earthquakes and famines and pestilence and wars... *there shall not an hair of our head perish.*[105] That takes care of our hair very nicely, even in moments of strife. But what of our lives in peacetime? And what about our food and drink and clothing? *Take no thought for your life, what you shall eat, or what you shall drink; nor yet for your body,*

---

[102] ibid. It is of interest since Epicurus was regarded to be an atheist.

[103] Hardly surprising since the word prayer comes from Latin *precaria*, from *precarius* meaning: obtained by begging, from *precari* to entreat.

[104] Matthew 10:30

[105] Luke 21:18

what you shall put on.[106] Sounds like a good deal for now, but what about tomorrow? *Take no thought for the morrow: for the morrow shall take thought for the things of itself.*[107] Let's see – that leaves...

That takes care of things pretty nicely, thank you!

[Aha! But what about "...whatsoever ye shall ask in my name, that will I do...?"[108] Hmmm. It can't have anything to do with food or drink or raiment, or life, or any future needs. Interesting.]

Yet this prayer business gets even worse. We are told that Kingdom of God (Heaven) is within us.[109] We are also told that our Father is in heaven. And the final stroke: "I and my Father are one".[110] In modern lingo, the Father is our Higher Self. It is our Spiritual Nature. [Or at the very least, our Higher Self in an indivisible part of the Father]. The Hebrews tried to tell us this with names like Eliah, Elijah, where *El* is the individualized spiritual presence, and *ah* or *jah* are abbreviations for *YHVE* or Yahveh, the Almighty, the Ineffable, the Eternal. Elijah means El and Yahveh are one, or, I and my Father are one. This is true, of course, for all who are convinced of their spiritual nature.

For all who are no longer dead.[111]

There may have been something in Plato's advice. The best advise we were given before Plato came from a psalmist who said: Keep still and know that I am God.[112] If we keep

---

[106] Matthew 6:25
[107] Matthew 6:34
[108] John 14:13
[109] Luke 17:21
[110] John 10:30
[111] Compare Matthew 8:22.
[112] Psalm 46:10

very, very still then maybe, just maybe, the fog shall be lifted from our eyes. It may be worth a try.

***

970106

*The Eternal has His intentions for all eternity.
If one prays to Him to do the contrary of what He has resolved,
it is praying Him to be weak,
frivolous, inconstant;
it is believing that He is thus, it is to mock Him.*

*In a word, we pray to God only because we have made Him in our own image. We treat Him like a pasha, like a sultan,
whom one may provoke and appease.*

Voltaire
[Fnaçois Marie Arouet]
1694 – 1778
THE PHILOSOPHICAL DICTIONARY
[transl. by H.I.Woolf; Knopf, 1924]

24

TRADITIONS

I've heard it said that every nation is proud of its traditions. This sentiment is often condensed to apply to individuals, groups and families, or extended to cover whole races. To protect our national traditions we go to war. We fight to protect our heritage. We fight for that which makes us different from others. We parade our differences as though the very fact that we are different had any bearing on the merit of that which sets us apart. On that which separates us. We – the good, versus "them" – the bad. We are always right. They – wrong.

Watching various groups bloating their meagre chests, one hears the word pride used often. They declare pride in their past. Pride in the accomplishments of those who went before them. Pride in being proud. "My father knew Lloyd George", said a nobody. "I am proud of being a female", asserts a feminist hating everyone who isn't. "I'm macho, a real man," counters a moron flexing his steroid muscles. I am proud of being a liberal, conservative, democrat, republican, communist, anarchist, any member of any group seeking power. I am proud of whatever it is that sets us apart.

That's *our* tradition, declares everyone needing support. Note, there is no such thing as *my* tradition. Traditionalists believe there is strength in numbers. They also need praise. In the absence of any individual accomplishment, it makes them proud.

We like to refer to our faltering pride as dignity. We are to be accorded human dignity, and then we are to die in dignity. The pope often spoke of the dignity of the common man. The Dalai Lama echoed the Holy Father's sentiments. Mother Theresa assures that people die with dignity. We hear that dignity is a basic human right. Workers have dignity. People strike with dignity. We are reminded of the dignity of a mother, a women. A child. Just about everyone has pride and is dignified. Dignity makes you feel important, importance make you feel proud.

Vanity of vanities, all is vanity, counters the Preacher.[113]

I feel neither proud nor dignified. I often like to behave in a most undignified manner. I like to fool around. I like to play childish games. I like ice cream. I like a good Disney cartoon. I like to have youthful, harmless fun. I also have no desire whatever to take credit for the accomplishments of my forefathers. Nor do I take pride in the accomplishments of those still living. Not even if I belong to the same sex, race, nation, family, political affiliation, professional body, age-group, or share the same disease.

I guess – I'm just not proud.

I am not proud of my racial or national traditions. I've done nothing to create them. I have done little to uphold them. I can hardly be proud of them. But I am also not ashamed of any of them. I am not ashamed of my heritage. I am not ashamed of it for the same reason that I am not proud of it. I had nothing to do with the agglomeration of either. The day I came into this world, I inherited an enormous bias. The Berlin wall fades in comparison to the barriers imposed on each and every one of us by our parents, schools, national governments, and religions. I don't know who is the most guilty. I suppose they all inherited their bias from their predecessors. Perhaps they can't be blamed for their heritage. For their traditions.

It is not easy to renounce one's past. It seems anchored in our genes. It is a part of us. Krishnamurti once said that

---

[113] ECCLESIASTES, or the Preacher.

"You can renounce a few cows, a house, but to renounce your heredity, your tradition, the burden of your conditioning, that demands an enormous inquiry".[114] The burden of our conditioning. But are we not more than Pavlovian dogs? If we must be proud, shouldn't it be of being endowed with a free will? Or are we all slaves to this insidious brainwashing we call traditions. The same sage, Krishnamurti, mused: "Freedom comes when the mind experiences without tradition."[115] Freedom! Surely, a word all but unknown to all steeped in traditions.

Again, the shackles of conditioning.

Conditioning requires a conditioner. One who imposes a condition. One who imposes that which *he* needs to lean on, to prop *himself* up against, lest *he* falls flat on the non-accomplishments of *his* own.

What if we decided to be proud only, ONLY, of our own accomplishments? If we stopped being proud of the great composers or painters, or philosophers who, by an accident of birth, had been spawned from a particular womb, in a particular country? Yet, there are no accidents. Nature disposes her greatest gifts not where most deserved (nature knows no national boundaries) but where most *needed*. Show me a nation where the creative spirit manifested itself in greatest abundance and I'll show you a nation capable of greatest depravity. Nature restores, or endeavours to maintain, balance.

Traditions are barriers that set us apart. No truly great man ever recognized boundaries. Greatest avatars, saviours, prophets, men and women, artists and scientists – they all gave to the world. Always, the *whole* world. The barriers are created by children of a lesser god. And those who create them are worshiped by immature owners of fragile egos.

---

[114] KRISHNAMURTI a biography by Pupul Jayakar (Harper & Row San Francisco)
[115] ibid.

I do not believe one must renounce one's heredity. Such sacrifice may be a noble, spiritual endeavour; it may be for the few, who choose this path. Perhaps they are the chosen few. But I do believe that being proud or ashamed of one's heritage is *non sequitur*. That pride nor shame do not follow nor result from one's ancestry, stock, lineage, pedigree or breeding. It may for champion dogs and cats, but nor for us. If we were to take pride in racial or national accomplishments, we would also be compelled to assume responsibility for racial or national crimes. All nations have skeletons in their cupboards. Mass murders, religious conversions at the point of a sword, persecutions of minorities, national cleansing, expropriations, usurping of land and its riches, theft on international scale. Buckminster Fuller wrote that: "the world came to identify history's most successful world-outlaw organization as the 'British Empire'".[116] History's heroes carry the burden of holocausts of every description. We build them monuments, adorn their brow with garlands of lotus leaves. We seem to forget that there are no proud nations. There are only proud people.

By choosing individuality, we choose freedom. I offer what little talent nature endowed me with – equally to all. No one should be proud of me. Nor must anyone take on the blame for my weaknesses. I shall carry my own burden, reap my own rewards. I am happy to share my successes, the burdens I shall keep to myself. They edify me. They cleanse me of pride.

We all carry some bias. We are children of tradition. I hope mine will die with me. I hope you will shed some of yours.

***

970110

---

[116] Fuller, R.Buckminster CRITICAL PATH [St.Marin's Press], pg.58.

25

THE MANY AND THE ONE

The needs of the many outweigh the needs of the one, said Mr. Spock, the taciturn science officer on the starship Enterprise. I wager that today, the needs of the many are far more sated by the innumerable variations on the Star Trek saga, then by our cultural heritage. Whatever our tastes or hunger, the sci-fi gender with a sprinkling of murder, sex and general mayhem seems to gratify our inner needs. We, on average, sleep eight hours, work and travel about ten, and for two hours we eat, drink and sip coffee. The rest of the time we watch television. Sci-fi, murder, sex and general mayhem. A daily conditioning. Brainwashing. We volunteer for our daily doze. Most of us, anyway.

And what of the arts? What of the heritage we're so proud of?

Where are the muses who led men on his search for the exquisite? Can Mnemosyne no longer bear any more daughters? Are Calliope, Euterpe, Erato and their noble sisters no longer guiding man in his search for beauty? Has even Apollo lost interest in his inspiring charges?[117]

---

[117] Zeus fathered nine of them. Their mother was Mnemosyne. Thy were: Calliope, Clio, Erato, Euterpe, Melpomene, Polyhymnia, Terpsichore, Thalia, and Urania. Their leader was Apollo.

The gods are dead! Says our Star Trek: we have outgrown them...

And as man entering the Age of Aquarius reaches out for his own immortality, he tramples on those who once were immortal. As man outgrows the gods of the past, the nine daughters of Zeus, he also seems to outgrow the divine traits that once made the muses immortal. We trample all that was once uplifting and sacred. We tramp on poetry in music, on harmony of light in the blend of colour, on balance and proportion in the works of sculpture, on firmness, commodity and delight in architectural structures. Man's literary efforts no longer attempt to inspire, to uplift, to share knowledge, but rather cater to the tastes of the many, to sate their need for fatuous satisfaction.

Irrevocably, wantonly, with gratuitous ease, the human race seems to regress to a neo-primitive state where escapism is no longer the domain of the drug-addict but the *modus vivendi* of the masses. It seems abundantly clear what are the needs of the many. The overriding need appears to be – escape. Escape from the reality created by us since we abandoned the search for beauty. Escape from the noble precepts once etched deeply in our derelict subconscious. Escape from the abysmal void bellowing in our empty hearts. Or so it seems. We killed our gods, burned their portentous altars. Now – we are alone.

The gods are dead. Long live the gods!
The needs of the gods always supersede the needs of the many.

There are cycles in vastness of the universe known as the Zodiac. It travels the sky in an endless procession of Equinoxes. The cycles, by human standards, are long. Each lasts over 2000 years. Each defines a completely new attribute that will be developed in man. Not in man's body. Not in his genes. In that aspect of man which is immortal.[118]

Our forefathers observed many other laws governing the universe, which appear immutable. One of them avers that one cannot affect a fundamental change in consciousness by partial adjustments.[119] The universe is designed in an extremely efficient manner. Nothing goes to waste – including effort. Apparently, when a new concept is presented to an individual consciousness (the soul) which is still harboring old notions, such a new concept is rejected. The soul is still conditioned, brainwashed, to impressions that served other, different lessons. Perhaps that is why humanity rejected Christianity. We didn't make a clean break from the old ways. We have been told to make *all* things new.[120] There are no half-measures possible. If we try to serve two authorities, we are left behind. We have been told all that. And have we listened? We continued to kill, to steal, to rob and exploit one another; many of us give our neighbour's wife or husband a glad eye – or we would, if we thought we could get away with it. We conduct wars, disparage each other's weakness; we certainly do not love one another. Not much, not often. And we do not keep the holy day holy, because most of us do not know what the word "holy" means. Could it be that we don't care enough to find out?

Let's face it. We are not *real* Christians.

Perhaps this is why the present Age of Aquarius is ruled by the planet Uranus. For what it's worth, Uranus is said to be a god that destroys the *status quo* to make room for his own influences. Perhaps all the gods are like that. Jealous gods. Perhaps that is why man destroys his gods to make

---

[118] See CYCLES, hereinbefore. The Zodiac actually spans c. 26,000 years, which allows approx. 2,167 years for each sign. The successive signs are link by lengthy overlapping periods.

[119] Compare Matthew 9:17. Wine symbolizes new knowledge, wineskins – our consciousness.

[120] "Behold, I make all things new" Revelation 21:5

room for himself. Regardless of the needs of the many, man must search for the needs of the one. Aquarians must tend their own garden, develop their own potential. Their own inner Self.

Or perhaps we must reach a long, long way back and rediscover our true home.

The idea of our divine origin had been planted in our subconscious at the dawn of history. The Greeks gave us Hercules – a human son of the gods who dared to confront his own creators. King David further defined our status almost 3000 years ago. From him we have learned that we *all* share divine origin.[121] A millennium later, Jesus repeated the same truth for our benefit.[122] Are we ready, at long last, to listen to the avatars?

So, finally, we have come of age. We reach boldly for the keys to our kingdom. We rejoice in accepting full responsibility for our lives. We know, from experience, that thoughts are "things", that every thought quickened with emotional energy will, sooner or later, becomes manifest in the physical universe. We have learned to control our thoughts. We are no longer weak underlings of kings, governments, the rich or the clergy. We blame no one for our lot, knowing full well that we, and we alone, have created the universe we live in. We don't even blame the stars. "It is not in our stars but in ourselves that we are underlings," said Cassius.[123] Like so many true poets, Shakespeare was a man born centuries ahead of his time.

And as we enter the kingdom of our newfound freedom we discover an even stranger truth. We needn't have fought

---

[121] Psalm 82:6 [Those who assign historical presence to David date his birth at 1040 B.C.]
[122] John 10:34
[123] Shakespeare, William JULIUS CÆSAR

so hard for our rights, our privileges, our riches, or any of our needs. The Kingdom and its riches are quite inexhaustible. Mr. Spock needn't have worried. We can put aside his quandary: the problem of the many and the one. No matter how many we are, in Truth, we are all but One.

***
970112

The soul, then, as being immortal...
and having seen all things that exist...
has knowledge of them all; and it is no wonder
that she should be able to call to remembrance all
that she ever knew about virtue,
and about everything;
for as all nature is akin, and the soul has learned
all things, there is no difficulty in her eliciting or
as men say learning, out of a single recollection
all the rest, if a man is strenuous
and does not faint;
for all enquiry and all learning is but recollection...

Socrates to Meno
[124]

---

[124] DIALOGUES OF PLATO [Random House, New York, 1937] pg. 360.

26

THE SHEPHERD & THE SHEEP

There are three methods of understanding the scriptures. There is the verbatim or literal interpretation favoured by the so-called Fundamentalists. This group probably still forms the largest segment of the Christian population. They ignore all logic, science, or even common sense, and insist that the scriptures are a direct, inerrant, word of God. They rely exclusively on faith, and when the evidence of their minds or senses contradicts their beliefs, the beliefs win. Many in this group like to be known as "Creationists", and they derive their anthropological and astrophysical knowledge from the Bible.[125] This group believes, for example, that the world was created in seven days, that Adam was put together "fully blown"[126] in 4004 BC, both to fit into the parameters and the time schedule of the fundamentalist's Bible. Most of the adherents of this group also believe that eventually the very same Adam will be bodily resurrected, presumably put together from the excretions of the bacteria which digested his remains aeons ago.

Not a pleasant prospect.

To the fundamentalists, not a word of the scriptures can be altered without incurring the risk of eternal damnation.[127]

---

[125] A cleric's defene of Galileo against the Catholic church that: "The purpose of Scripture is to teach how one goes to heaven, not how heaven goes" – fell of deaf ears.

[126] An expression used by a southern Baptist, in a telecast, who confessed to being a "Creationist".

[127] I understand this to be true of the adherents of the Bible as well as other Scriptures.

Their God demands absolute obedience and those who confess allegiance to Him insist on absolute obedience from their own flock. Their leaders lay claim to infallibility in the matters of faith. When disparity exists between science and (their interpretation of) the scriptures, science is judged to be wrong. The Christian believers in this group often liken themselves to the sheep of the Lord, Lord God, an omnipotent, jealous deity who demands total submission. To assure conformity to their interpretation of the scriptures, the fundamentalists invented tangible, "real", though not geographically determined, heaven and hell, destinations that stretch (time-wise) forever. The satisfaction they seek is almost exclusively emotional. The Christian members of this group invariably address their prayers to the second person of the Holy Trinity, the Son, whom they recognize as their Shepherd.

The second group are those who insist that the human mind is a gift of God – though perhaps not the same God as that venerated by the previous group. This God is more than a tyrannical superhuman entity that metes out graces and punishments to all that obey or disobey His laws. This group recognizes the paradoxes in the Bible as parables, allegories, introduced by the (inspired) seers and scribes, to facilitate the understanding of metaphysical concepts. They do believe, however, that there is tremendous wisdom and beauty in the scriptures, which, in spite of many distortions resulting from many (often manual) rewrites over the centuries, still serve to assist man in his search for his purpose.

The members of this group are usually well educated. They enjoy indulging in disciplined research to find the truth that might not be immediately apparent. They are well-read and like to dig below the surface. They rely on their minds (rather than emotions) and, to a considerable degree, seek intellectual satisfaction. Their search for the truth is seldom limited to the scriptures. They find all philosophies worthy and tempting morsels for their intellectual hunger. They are no longer sheep to be led by a good shepherd. If anything, they would rather be shepherds themselves, though they are apt to ignore all who do not share their rational approach. When members of this group indulge in prayer, they address the first member of the Trinity, whom they recognize as the Universal Mind.

The third and last group is the hardest to define.

They may or may not be well educated. They may or may not rely on their faith to the exclusion of all else. They do not believe that any particular scripture is an exclusive source of divine knowledge. They refuse to place restrictions on the efficacy of the Holy Spirit. They believe that the scriptures offer *spiritual* rather than historical, geographical or scientific knowledge. They also believe that the Truth is not really hidden, that it is available to all seekers. They tend to think that the truth will eventually reach all ears. That it is only a question of time and, since souls are immortal, there is no hurry.

The members of this group will not hide their beliefs but they will not impose them on others either. They would not preach because they usually believe that the Truth manifests itself through every vessel differently. That, though Truth is One, we can only approach it subjectively. They also believe that when we are stripped of our physical, mental and emotional bodies, what is left is immortal, indestructible, universal. That nothing the members of the first two groups do, or don't do, can in any way affect them, injure them, do them any harm. They believe that they are not human beings endowed with an immortal soul. They believe that they are immortal soul that is temporarily acquiring knowledge in the physical universe.

Most of us fit somewhere on the periphery of one of the

above groups. Those who don't are going through a relatively short phase known as apostasy. This phase, or condition, is necessary, since mixing of the above groups is almost impossible. Human consciousness refuses to accept contradictory concepts. Dichotomy is painful. If we submit to our fate, we find our niche somewhere in the first group. We grin and bear our cross. We suffer, but we must. If, within our reality, God 'told' us to press a button of mass destruction, we would do it. We submit to the will of our God. We do not rationalize, we obey. We rely on faith and faith alone.

If we rebel against the external world we are probably in the middle group. We are fighters. We no longer fight with our fists, nor weapons of mass destruction. The word, for us, is mightier than the sword. We despise all that is irrational, because it insults our intellectual opinion of our own worth, which is usually a mite inflated.

And what of the last group?

They try not to fight any battles. They know that fight is a symptom of a dualistic reality. They fear nothing, so they have no need to fight. They also tend to submit to their God, but their God is one that has no interest in this world. To them the material universe is not the true reality. In their temporary sojourn on earth, God neither punishes nor rewards them. There are laws and these laws take care of all that is. These people tend to be observers. They believe that while the seeker and the observer are one, they must give free rein to the seeker. They alternate consciousness with the seeker. Sometimes they are the observers, sometimes the observed. It is a process of learning. Occasionally they help the seeker. Gently, by prodding rather than insisting. They have few ambitions other than to observe and learn.

In a way, they are the shepherd *and* the sheep. Two in one. Sometimes.

***

970114

27

MYTH AND REALITY

The treasury of myths abounds in the world. It abounds in our subconscious, fills our dreams, controls our behaviour through subliminal impulses seldom questioned by our waken awareness. All worldly religions are shrouded in myth. Man's need for heroes to worship is matched by his inability to live without them. These beacons are as necessary to man's souls as food is to his body.

The myths engulfing Christianity are as varied as the denominations themselves. The summary of the basic doctrines is contained in the Creed, a derivative of the Latin word: credo, meaning – I believe. But even there we find a gradual evolution of tenets. Churches do not rule by tradition alone. Traditions change, dogmas are adapted and implemented. The original Nicene Creed was a concise statement and included a declaration on the nature of Christ. This Creed of the First Council of Nicæa in 325, has been revised at the First Council of Constantinople in 381, to settle problems raised by Arianism.[128] Much later, a 9th century addition by the Catholic Church stating that: "the Holy Ghost procedeth

---

[128] Briefly: Arianism [from theologian priest Arius] proposed a Son who was not equal with the Father. The dispute became political with whole groups of bishops being exiled by emperors.

from the Father *and* the Son",[129] led to antagonism with the Orthodox Eastern Church.

In the meantime, the battle against Arianism continued, and in the 6th century the Catholic Church adopted a new statement. This creed is known as the Athanasian Creed and reinforces the belief in the Trinity and the Incarnation.[130]

Next we come to the so called: Apostles' Creed, familiar to most conservative churches. While its origin dates back to 2nd or 3rd century, its present form was reached only in the 7th century. It is simpler than the Nicene Creed, but differs in two significant statements: it purports that Christ descended into hell, and it proposes a "resurrection of the body", rather than the "resurrection of the dead", avowed in the Nicene version. As Christ's descent into hell is not to be found in earlier manuscripts, the idea was probably an interpolation from the fables of Bacchus and Hercules and adopted as an article of Christian faith.[131] A similar comment would apply to the myth of the resurrection of Osiris, Adonis, Bacchus, and other sun-gods in Pagan religions. Strangely enough, the credo being recited in the Catholic mass in Vatican, states "Et exspecto ressurectionem *mortuorum* ", i.e. it affirms the resurrection of the dead, not of the body. Since Jesus called dead those not yet spiritually awakened[132], one wonders why was this distortion of a "bodily" resurrection allowed to entangle the faithful. On purpose? Why wasn't it yet rectified? Since the theory of the Mass was formally de-

---

[129] Et in Spiritum Sanctum, Dominum et vivificantem, qui ex Patre *Filioque* procedit.

[130] This creed is named after Saint Athanasius, a patriarch of Alexandria at the time of his vigorous opposition to Arianism during the 4th century.

[131] Gleamed from ISIS UNVEILED II - by H.P.Blavatsky (Theosophical University Press) pg. 177

[132] Matthew 8:22 or John 11:25

MYTH AND REALITY 133

fined by the year 1215,[133] surely, there must have been ample time. Could it have something to do with an attempt to keep the masses (faithful) ignorant? And if so, why?

In the interests of "why", I've attempted to separate the myth from the fact promulgated in the creed. Since the Apostles' creed is adopted by most denominations, I shall use it as an illustration.

> *I believe in God the Father Almighty, Maker of heaven and earth; and in* **Jesus** *Christ his only Son, our Lord,* **who was** *conceived by the Holy Ghost,* **born of** *the Virgin* **Mary, suffered under Pontius Pilate, was crucified, died, and buried**; *he descended into hell; the third day he rose from the dead; he ascended into Heaven, and sitteth at the right hand of God, the Father Almighty; from thence he shall come to judge the quick and the dead. I believe in the Holy Ghost; the holy Catholic Church; the communion of saints; the forgiveness of sins; the resurrection of the body; and the life everlasting.*[134]

In bold lettering are, to the best of our knowledge, facts. The rest – printed in italic – myths. For almost one billion people these myths are a powerful emotional drug.[135] Once absorbed into the psyche, it is extremely difficult to revert to a rational stance. Yet, in addition to all the above, we also have the Augsburg Confession of the Lutherans, the Thirty-nine Articles of the Anglican and Episcopal churches, the Westminster Confession of the Calvinists – basic to Presby-

---

[133] WESTERN CIVILIZATIONS by Edward McNall Burns (8h Edition Volume 1) pg. 227
[134] THE APOSTLES' CREED [Philip Schaff, The Creeds of Christendom (New York, Harper and Brothers 1884)
[135] I believe it was Marx or perhaps Lenin, who called religion the opium of the masses.

terianism and Congregationalism, and probably many others. And these are only the Christian creeds. What of countless other religions?

And when all is said and done, we are left with a vision. The vision reveals to John a cross of light, and explains that "I have suffered none of the things which they will say of me; even that suffering which I showed to you and to the rest of my dance, I will that it be called a mystery."[136]

***

970116

> "Therefore, since it has been demonstrated that
> the self-moving principle is eternal,
> the same must be applied to the human soul....
> ....Since the soul possesses this characteristic of
> self motion,
> we can only conclude that it too, has no beginning
> and lives for ever."

Marcus Tullius Cicero
106 – 43 B.C.
THE DREAM OF SCIPIO
[Translated from the Latin by Richard Hooker]

---

[136] Pagels Elaine H. [Apocryphon of John II, The GNOSTIC GOSPELS [Vintage Books, div. of Random House, New York] pg.89/90

28

THE CARROT & THE STICK

Heaven and hell. The ultimate carrot – the ultimate stick. Goethe, Dante, Mann, Milton, Verdi, Boîto, Gounod, Liszt.... They, and countless others, explored the euphoria of paradise and the ultimate depravity of hell. To the mystics, philosophers, artists, composers and poets, such concepts are expressions of states of consciousness. To the religious, they stand for the ultimate if inexplicable, virtually unattainable happiness, and eternal suffering with no hope of reprieve. It is indeed a depraved god who would impose, on his beloved children, the latter. No matter – perhaps, it is only a stick. Never mind that such an idea was foreign to the ancient Jews or Greeks; the Christian churches, all too soon, found hell a very convenient stick.

Paradise was far harder to explain as a prospective carrot.

Most people find it much easier to imagine being permanently miserable than permanently happy. And the churches were at a loss to explain how can sitting on a cloud with a harp under your arm is supposed to compensate us for the loss of goodies which we are encouraged to part from: the churches being the obvious beneficiaries. Nevertheless, this premise became an amazing ecclesiastic achievement, considering that there is absolutely no mention in the Bible of giving any church any money, whatever. Indeed, the gospels encourages giving *all* to the poor, and surely, no one, in their wildest dreams, could possibly confuse the church with the poor.[137] The Babylonian riches of Vatican will surely attest to that. The fact, however, that there were no churches in biblical times, may have had something to do with it. It was later that St. Paul did his best to organize one, but even he didn't get very far. By the end of the first century, "thirty sects of Christians might be reckoned in Asia Minor, in Syria, in Alexandria, and even in Rome".[138] Evidently, with heaven in abeyance and with hell's topography not defined, it could not have been easy to train the early Christians. Perhaps they were teaching something quite different from the teaching of today.

So far: no carrot and no stick.

But the good theologians soon took care of this obvious deficiency. The Valley of (the son of) Hinnom was quickly 'transliterated' into Greek as *gehanna,* and into English as hell. The same translation was allotted to the Hebrew *Sheol* (the unseen state), the Greek *Tartarus, Hades,* and probably any other word that would serve as a half-decent stick. A sort of mass-produced idea of eternal damnation. And the stick had to be powerful. A Catholic theologian, Tillemont, summed up the idea rather well. He wrote: "all the illustrious Pagans are condemned to the eternal torments of hell, because they lived before the time of Jesus, and, therefore, could not be benefited by the redemption".[139] Voilà! That took care of the opposition in a nice clean sweep.

That also took care of hell, er... the stick, very nicely. But what of heaven?

Not quite as easy.

---

[137] Nor should those who benefited from the taxation known as tithing be confused with the church. Note, that should there have been twenty tribes, the "tithe" would have been around one-twentieth, rather than one-tenth.

[138] THE TRADITIONS OF THE WESTERN WORLD (Rand McNally) Voltaire: Toleration, pg. 402

[139] ISIS UNVEILED (II Theology) H.P. Blavatsky pg.8

But the human brain is a marvelous instrument when it comes to carrots. Furthermore, necessity is a mother of invention. Since hell no longer referred to a state of mind (a state of consciousness which has temporarily lost its awareness of God's presence), surely one can equally pervert the obverse condition. Rather than accepting Christ's concept that heaven is a state of mind, that the Kingdom of God is within our consciousness[140], let us see what we can do with the concept that heaven is only attainable after death. This peccadillo has many advantages. One, we no longer have to give it any psychological, not to mention geographical, topography. We can say that only God knows what heaven is like, and He wont tell us. We must also make sure that not too many people will read the New Testament, which, unfortunately, is full of similitudes of heaven. But with the world being predominantly illiterate, that's the least of our problems.

Almost there!

But not quite. If both heaven and hell are to become exclusively a carrot and a stick, than we must find a way to *wield* both. Or at least the stick! By now, after the successful perversions of heaven and hell, this was easy. All the Orthodox Church had to do was to convince people that God gave St. Peter power to speak in His name, and that the church has exclusive copyrights to this idea. Two elements were necessary. One, Jesus had to become God. This although the Christ claimed to be the *Son of* God, and was willing to share this honour with others. Don't believe me? Look it up in John 10:34. This didn't serve the purpose. Jesus had to become the *only* Son of God. And, as such, inserted into the official Creed. The Gnostics, the Cerinthians, the Arianists, and many others rebelled against it. But that was no longer a problem. The stick was now all-powerful. The opposition was simply anathematized (excommunicated) or exiled. Lots and lots of

---

[140] compare Luke 17:21, Romans 14:17

them. The little guys and the bishops.[141] *En masse.* The church now had the tools to build an empire. It may have taken a little longer for the faithful to accept that St. Peter (who three times in a single night denied any knowledge of Jesus) was to be His successor, but... we are only human.

The carrot and the stick were now ready!

But... someone, along the way, forgot yet another statement of Jesus: "Go ye therefore, and *teach* all nations"[142]. Not go and *train* them, like Pavlovian dogs or circus seals, with a carrot and a stick. Not go a scare the living daylights out of them while robbing them of their possessions.... But *teach* all nations.

Oops!

We are back at the starting gate.

Perhaps, one day, the Christian churches will start teaching their faithful to love one another; teaching them that heaven is within one's heart. When that happens, they might notice that no great teacher ever, EVER, employed a carrot or a stick. Heaven and hell will, once again, become states of consciousness.

I rather think that we are not here to teach each other but to learn *from* one another. By example. By observation. Are we not all children of the most High?[143] And furthermore, the rate of personal growth is a direct result *not* of someone's capacity to teach, but of *our* capacity to learn. All we need is just a little help.

Just a little help....

***

970117

---

[141] THE COLUMBIA VIKING DESK ENCYCLOPEDIA 3rd. Ed.: Arianism: (Arius c.256-336) "The conflict went on, with whole groups of bishops being exiled by emperors..."
[142] Matthew 28:19
[143] Psalm 82:6

29

VANISHING WORLDS

I had a vision. In it, each man and woman was a universe interconnected with every other man and woman by that which they each held in common. That shared or objective universe was but a tiny fraction of the richness of ideas, thoughts, dreams, hopes, which fermented within their individual minds. But it was objective. It was that which was common to most of them. It was that which they agreed on. It was a point of reference. That's all. Just a point of reference.

A critical mass of shared ideas determines the universe detectable by our senses.

In the past, such old, now dissolved worlds, had been handed down to us as lore: MU, Lemuria, Atlantis, had all been very real to the men and women who inhabited those conglomerates of ideas, we call an objective universe. As we progress, evolve, the subjective mind rejects the old to make room for the new. Most people find it difficult to accept that Lemuria or Atlantis ever existed.

Well, they did, but not in the way we imagine.

Could our glorious universe cease to exist, as did the worlds of our past? The stars, galaxies... trees, flowers... mountains and oceans... the human heritage of culture, civilizations? Was the earth once flat? Could a sailor fall over the edge – if he believed in it hard enough? Does an adamant, unshakeable faith have the power to create reality? Or is it always the same, tired, polluted, exploited, eternal universe – with only us changing....

No, surely this could never be.

Generations of men speculated on the immortality of soul. Later, on prolongation of physical life, of our material bodies. This is the phase we live in at the present. We shall genetically engineer our bodies to last in them a mite longer. Perhaps another twenty, or fifty, or maybe another hundred years. And then what? We all seem to suffer from an insatiable hunger for permanency, for continuity. Why?

In my vision... well, judge for yourselves.

First I was shown the ancient civilization of MU where now the barren sands of the Gobi desert guard the primordial secrets. Or so I thought! Later I saw the dissolution of Lemuria (were we the lemuroid primates?) supposedly in or under the Pacific or the Indian Ocean. Finally, the mighty Atlantis, where inter-planetary travel was as common as jet planes are today, had been swallowed beneath the turbulent waves of the Atlantic. But have you noticed that with all our superb technology, which allowed us to put a man on the moon, does not aid us in discovering even a single iota of those past universes? No, my friend, the Gobi desert hides no secrets, the depth of the oceans do not secrete past civilizations.

Oh, they did exist – but not where we presume them to have been.

We place them in those inaccessible locations to hide them from our ineptness of not being able to locate them in our objective universe. But in the oceans of today, of the present, they never existed. No more than our world will exist after the end of the present procession of equinoxes. Every 52,000 years, every double grand cycle of the Zodiac, our psyche takes a gigantic leap into the unknown.[144] The leap is so fantastic that, had we been able to retain the memories of previous experiences, our mind would not only reject them, but we would get seriously... unhinged. Perhaps stark, raving, mad.

But you don't have to worry.

When the time comes, we shall once again start at the bottom rung of the ladder. We shall enter Eden with joy in our hearts, with untrammelled faith that this, new Eden shall last forever. It almost will. Every golden age is by far the longest. We shall be spared the knowledge that silver, and bronze and the iron ages will follow. They don't have to, but... such is our nature.

We shall always strive to be gods, creators. Our minds shall crave knowledge even as our bodies crave physical sustenance. We shall always reach out for the stars...

But these changes will only happen when we are ready. Then the critical mass of people will make the next objective universe come into being. Yet even then, some, whose minds cannot shed archetypal memories hidden in the bottomless pit of their subconscious, shall create legends of the universes past. Some will try desperately to reach back in time. Back to an all but forgotten reality. But the critical mass, perhaps even majority, after aeons of dabbling with the creative surges welling in our ever-expanding consciousness, shall become drunk with power. We shall come to regard the objective worlds as real universes, as worlds of substance.

---

[144] Twice the 12 signs. Each sign is represented in the Bible by a particular patriarch. St.John the Divine writes in the Revelation 4:10, "and round about the throne were four and twenty seats: and upon the seats I saw four and twenty elders sitting..." The importance of this number of 24 is evident since it appears in 4:10, 5:8, 5:14, 11:16, and 19:4. Emmet Fox in ALTER YOUR LIFE, [Harper and Row] pg.116 writes: "we have been twice around the Zodiac since we last made such a giant step forward as the present one."

And when we stray too far... an avatar shall be send to us. He will remind us that the True reality is a state of consciousness. It exists only within our hearts. That we all, every one of us, create the ephemeral universe we live in. That the material reality is an illusion, that it is transient, that, in time, it will dissolve itself. That it will vanish. He will remind us that the True Reality is never physical, material, but that It has its Being within the realm of the infinite potential, of inexhaustible ideas. By telling us the Truth, He will attempt to free us from our neurotic attachment to our past anchored in our own creations. We shall sense the Truth and listen to Him carefully, but the price of freedom will be too high for our egos. We would have to give up our illusory world. Our creation. So we shall crucify Him.

Just wait and see....

***

970121

30

THE STRANGER

The stranger sat down opposite me at *my* table. I was a bit taken aback as the café was half-empty. I was ready to change tables myself, to protect my "psychic space", when the stranger, seemingly reading my thoughts said: "Please stay". For reasons not quite clear to me I remained in my seat.

"I do not mean to impose, but I need information," the stranger said. All the time his eyes were riveted to mine. There seemed both kindness and power in them, but most off all there was serenity. It was like looking into the smoothest of the blue skies, or perhaps into the depth of an ocean. An ocean of peace.

"How can I help you?" I asked. I wasn't really mollified at his invasion of my privacy but I was just a little curious.

"I don't know." The eyes now looked right through me, before focusing on my own irises once again. "I want to know what happened... " The sentence was left unfinished but the stranger remained silent.

"With what...? I prompted. The silence stretched. I wanted to glance at my watch but, somehow, I found it inappropriate. The time seemed to have diluted, receded into a secondary awareness.

"...with the world, I suppose? With the people." His eyes had a disconcerting habit of oscillating between some nondescript distant horizon and the very centres of my pupils. It felt almost as if he couldn't make up his mind.

"People? What people?" My question was again met with silence. I tried again: "Well, you know, people are people. They never change. I mean, not really, do they?" I felt compelled to prompt the man. In spite of myself, I sensed that his questions were, in some way, pertinent. If I could only find out, pertinent to what?

"Don't they?"

That's it. He was good at saying very little. It wasn't my forte. "Well, you know, they don't really. The goodish ones are goodish, the bad ones pretty bad..." His eyes again drifted beyond the horizon. "...it's always like that. As long as I can remember. You get born, you grow up, you get a job, you have children, they leave home, you get bored, you die?" Half way through my sentence I thought I was being flippant. Somewhere along I realized I wasn't.

"Do you?"

"Do I what?" This guy was unreal. If it weren't for my having a half-hour to kill – and for his eyes – I would have been out of there. "Do I what!" I repeated.

"Die."

"Listen, if I bore you, you can sit over there." My voice rose a couple of decibels, before I simmered down. "Where are you from, anyway?" The man was not easy to get annoyed with – too much serenity in those eyes – but I had no idea what was his problem. His accent was completely nondescript.

"Why do people die?" The stranger asked softly.

The man was on a different time-track. He *was* unreal. I decided to give him one last chance. "Everybody dies. There are diseases, accidents, fights, murders, wars. Everybody dies. For crying our loud, even Jesus died!"

THE STRANGER

For the first time he lowered his gaze to the table. There followed a long silence. Finally, as if coming back from far, far away, he said two words: "Did he?"

I can play this game as well as anybody. "Didn't He?"

"No."

"And I suppose He wasn't crucified either, right?" I think I got him.

"You mean his body being nailed to the cross, and all that?"

"And all that!? You're not very respectful, are you?" I thought of myself as a good Christian. I didn't approve of people taking liberties with my faith. Or anybody's, for that matter.

"Did they listen to his teaching?" He didn't apologize.

"Who, I mean whose?"

"Did the people listen to that man's, ah... Jesus' teaching?" He asked very quietly. In fact I could swear his lips weren't moving.

"What's the matter with you, man? You've been in a deep freeze the last 2000 years? Of course they listened. Christianity is the largest religion in the world. Or at least as big as Islam. And even they recognize Jesus as a great prophet." I felt obliged to give credit where credit was due.

"And people still die?"

As I've already said, this guy was unreal. If it weren't for his eyes, I would have thought he escaped from the local loony farm.

"Just what has one thing got to do with another?" This would get him on the run.

"Didn't this Jesus say that if you believe in him you will never die?"

I was no expert on the Bible, but this expression the stranger quoted did strike me as familiar. I felt sure it was in one of the gospels. I'd have to look it up. One day. "He may have said it, but..." It was my turn to give him the silent treatment. What a hell was I suppose to say anyway? By now

I felt sure that Jesus did say those very words. "There is believing and believing..." I countered lamely.

"...and though he were dead, he shall live again. Did people believe in that?"

His eyes were dead centred on mine. I was sure that he knew my answer before I opened my mouth. But this time, I knew, I had him in the corner. "Sure," I was on safe ground, "we all believe in the resurrection of the body!"

"What body?" For the first time there was real amusement in the stranger's eyes. "You mean the dust you wrap around your soul?"

"Dust?" My turn to be monosyllabic.

"Never mind." The amusement ebbed. "So people still die... " The horizon was out in full force. "I suppose it's not time yet." He said in a flat monotone.

"Time for what?" I prodded. The man talked in riddles.

"Time for the next... for the second... stage." The piercing look, the horizon, the serenity were all gone. The agony in the man's eyes pressed down on me like a thousand tons of bricks. This must be what hell is like, I thought.

"Is s-s-something w-w-wrong?" I stammered. Thank God it only lasted a second. I wiped my forehead. I've never witnessed such pain.

"Is there anything I can do for you?" The stranger asked. The serenity was back.

I was still recovering. I took a deep breath. "Who are you?" Suddenly it became important.

"I?" And for the first time an enigmatic smile lightened the man's face. "I am you. We are all one. Really. Do you believe that?"

***

970124

31

THE STAGE

I am but and actor, and the world is my stage. Was it Shakespeare who said that? Whoever it was, he was right. The world is a stage on which we enact our little dramas, comedies, and, if we are very unlucky, our tragedies.

Actually, the roles we play have nothing to do with luck. Luck is what the weak blame for their misfortunes. The bard I quoted also said: "It is not in our stars but in ourselves that we are underlings".[145] If we only knew that our season on this stage is no more than a brief stint, tailored-made to learn a very specific lesson, we would not take our roles, not to mention ourselves, quite so seriously.

Some of us discover the role we are supposed to play early. This discovery is called self-realization. People lucky enough to make this discovery are those who fulfil their purpose in life. They are the few, the chosen. Or perhaps, they just looked harder. They come in all walks of life but they have one thing in common. They are a happy lot.

But until we discover our purpose, the role we are supposed to play, we take part in various productions. First we are allotted the roles of children. Most of us are very good at that, although even this category seems to be split into the nice, well-behaved children, and.... the obnoxious brats. The latter group really comes into its own during the rapacious

---

[145] Shakespeare, William JULIUS CÆSAR [Cassius addressing Brutus].

teen-years. The know-it-all-teen, the don't-tell-me-what-to-do-teen, the how-come-you-can-and-I-can't-teen. There are many variations on the theme. I refer to these years as rapacious, because they subsist on greed and prey. They claim what is not theirs, what they haven't earned. Their demands are not integral to their consciousness. This, in fact, is the first, indispensable lesson for all of us.

And then we come of age. We start performing our adult roles. We step on this audacious stage somewhere between our middle twenties and late sixties. Assuming, we ever do, of course. According to Winston Churchill, some of us crossover from juvenile delinquency directly to sterile senility. Some of us never go through the stage of adulthood.

Not us, of course. We are all very mature. Right? Then why do we act as animals, emotional dunces, pseudo-intellectuals and even as saints – on occasion. Surely, most of us do indulge in these passing fancies. Don't we?

An average adult (that's us) has to juggle several roles at once. The stage of life is much more demanding than a theatrical illusion. Nevertheless, most of us must perform our roles of understanding, loving husbands-wives, strictish but affectionate fathers-mothers, self-abating breadwinners-homemakers (often both), obedient employees, responsible bosses, compassionate neighbours and, if we are very undeserving: important personages. Now, as long as we remain firmly committed to role playing, all's well and good. The problems start when we forget that we are on a stage. When we do forget, all hell breaks loose.

First we begin taking the world seriously – then ourselves. We confuse the stage with the permanent reality and ourselves with the roles we play. We forget that we keep rotating our roles all the time, to make sure this cannot happen, but – it still does.

To most of us. Sometimes.

So what can we do when this happens? What is our retreat from this pathological condition? Can we run, escape, step on another stage? Can we fight this mirage? How many times have we all asked ourselves: "How could I have been so stupid?" "So irresponsible?" "So ungrateful for the blessings all around me?"

The answer is as simple as it is unexpected: Nothing.

Assuming we recognize our condition as one in which we do not wish to remain, we have to do absolutely nothing. Whatever role we are emoting, and that's all it is, *overacting*, the particular part, scene or play will dissolve – the moment we stop thinking about it. If we feel guilty, ashamed, angry with our fate, the world, husband, wife, boss or whatever, we shall only prolong the scene we got stuck in.[146] If, on the other hand, we simply sit back and wait for the stupid condition to pass – it will. We shall either earn applause or some boos, but that is the worst that can happen. Providing that we do nothing. This is the glory of being an actor: we can always improve on our performance the *next* time. But if we try to improve a bad performance while emoting, i.e.: if we fight evil, we give it reality. That is what evil is: a false image, mirage, maya, being mistaken for reality. By fighting it, we make it so real that we, ourselves, begin to believe in it.

We fight windmills.

Fortified with this knowledge, we can play any part we choose. We can, and should, play our role as best we can. We must try to give a Royal Command Performance every time. But we should never forget that we are only on a stage. That our true reality is not the theatre but, what Deepak Chopra called, the Field of Infinite Possibilities.[147] A Stage of Infinite

---

[146] There are 4 principle symptoms of alienation from True Reality: 1, we feel bad, depressed; 2, nobody seems to understand us, we feel left out, apart; 3, we feel a great need for a change (i.e.: an escape from the false reality); 4, we tend to blame others for our condition.

[147] Chopra, Deepak AGELESS BODY, TIMELESS MIND [Harmony Books, div. of Crown Publ.]

Parts. Every actor's paradise!

Since we all are masters of our own universes, everything and everybody in our own, personal universe is exactly what we believe them to be. It cannot be otherwise. We, and only we, can create our own reality. If it weren't so, the scriptures would hardly call us gods! Right? We create not only our parts, but also the stage, the audience the theatre itself. For a while. It is always only for a while.

We are immortal, but the plays are transient, ephemeral. Once we truly accept this concept, we shall never worry about over-acting again. Because even if we do emote, emotionalize, sentimentalize, carry on, rage, rant... once in a while, well, it is only a play. A drama, a comedy or even a tragedy, in an endless procession of plays. And roles. So we might as well enjoy our parts, our dramas. The world is but a stage. And let us not forget... we are also the directors!

Break a leg!

***

970125

32

FAITH

"**Credo, quia impossible est**" – I believe, because it is impossible.[148] In this statement John Locke draws a firm barrier between Faith and Reason.[149] On this false premise the churches had built their power over the faithful. On this premise the faithful have been duped into believing in whatever their common sense told them is impossible. A very fallacious premise.

Why should anyone believe in the impossible? Why should anyone accept that some people have a better connection into the library of celestial or esoteric knowledge then others? Have those who claim that privilege proven their thesis? Did anyone of them ever demonstrate that their knowledge is in anyway superior to the knowledge of others? If you can answer yes to anyone of the above – believe them. If not...? Perhaps the Almighty gave us brains in order for us to use them. Not to rely on blind faith.

So what is Faith, anyway?

Webster Dictionary defines it as *unquestioning belief.*

---

[148] John Locke: An Essay Concerning Human Understanding (Chicago: Henry Regnery Co., 1956)
[149] John Locke's (1632-1704) critique of Descartes thesis revolutionized the current views ranging from aesthetics to education and religious toleration.

Why *unquestioning*, it doesn't say, but Mr. Webster elaborates, inter alia, *unquestioning belief in God*. Again, I ask, why unquestioning? Surely, by questioning the very existence of God – assuming God really does exists – we can only discover this Entity more profoundly. Are we to be afraid that if we question God's existence, He will disappear?

Paul the Apostle claims that faith is the substance of things hoped for, the evidence of things not seen.[150] The phrase would sound better if the Greek word were to be correctly translated as substratum, or: what *stands under*, rather than "substance". If faith were to be a substratum, it would act as a motivator, a catalyst. Certainly not a blind act, or feeling, abrogating any and all mental activity. As for the "evidence" of things not seen, the Greek word *elegchos could* also be translated as *conviction*, but either way is sounds like an oxymoron. After all, who cares if the "things" are seen or not if there is sufficient "evidence" to prove with conviction that they exist? Whenever I read the scriptures I must constantly remind myself that they were written at a time when a vast majority of people could neither read nor write. Furthermore, the words may well have changed their meaning considerably during the last 2000 years. Sometimes, only the poetry remains – with the spiritual knowledge hidden deep within.

But back to Faith.

Elsewhere, Paul lists three virtues that he finds indispensable to (presumably a happy) life. These are: Faith, Hope, and Charity. Of these, he relegates faith to a secondary position, indicating that charity is the greatest of the three[151]. Interesting. Enough said that if we rely on the Bible, we are

---

[150] Hebrews 11:1
[151] 1 Corinthians 13:13

FAITH

given choice galore, and a few contradictions to boot.[152]

Perhaps life would be a lot easier, if we stopped treating the Bible as an infallible religious document, and attempted to use it for enlightenment. I am reminded of a saying that we use the Bible as a drunk uses a lamppost. For support, not for illumination. And how does this help us with the question of faith?

Substantially.

If we assume that the Bible is a document that endeavours to sum up the treasury of human knowledge which, when put into practice, will enhance our lives, than we gain a tremendous freedom of interpretation. And freedom, surely, is a divine trait. Every one of us can examine how the wisdom of the Bible applies to his or her individual life. Not how it applies to any group of sermonizers who wish to impose their exegesis on us. Secondly, we can play down the exclusivity of the "divine nature" of the Bible, since *all* knowledge, surely, comes from the same source. Why? Because there is only one Source. How do I know? I observe the evidence of the things not seen!

Seriously though. From now on, we can question what we read instead taking it on blind faith. All we have to accept is that faith is a necessary ingredient of our life. When I stand up, I have faith that I shall not fall over on becoming erect. I can't be 100% sure of it, but I have faith in the ability of my legs to support me. Once, I had one-too-many and I was wrong. Now I temper my faith with some evidence.

Faith is the most indispensable catalyst for action and progress. Every scientist attempting to open new horizons of knowledge must believe that he will, or at the very least

---

[152] Compare: "What doth it profit, my brethren, though a man say he hath faith, and have not works? can faith save him?" (James 2:14) versus "Therefore we conclude that a man is justified by faith without the deeds of the law." (Romans 3:28) Take your choice.

might, succeed. Otherwise, he would be a fool to even try. No man nor woman could carry out thousands of experiments, burning midnight oil over many years, if they were not motivated by faith in eventual success. Faith in eventual success. And what's more, their faith must be renewed every time they go to the lab. That's a lot of faith! Whenever we venture into the unknown, whatever it might be, faith is our dynamic. Without it we would all be still sitting in our caves or cringing on the upper branches of the jungle. Faith brought us down from the trees; faith has lifted us up to the moon. If we could only disassociate faith from religion, perhaps we could all take flight on the wings of our imagination. And then, having enough faith in our potential, we could actually make our wings real.

To paraphrase Paul: Faith is the beginning, the fuse, the ignition. Hope is what keeps the process going (though Faith still sustains us). Charity is the creative process itself. It is not the lover that matters, nor the loved one. It is Love itself that is the expression of the Divine. But none of it can happen if we have no faith.

***
970128

And now abideth faith, hope, charity, these three;
but the greatest of these is charity.

1 Corinthians 13:13

33

YE ARE GODS

What did the psalmist mean by this statement? Who are these "ye"? What do they look like, how do they act, what are their characteristics? What would you be like if the above expression applied to you? If you claim to be a Jew, or a Christian, or of a different faith, or of no faith at all, you may still find the biblical thesis intriguing. Alternatively, you might find it superbly challenging to develop your own definition of divinity. The skies are the limit. Or the heavens. Take your pick.

On the other hand, it may be of no interest to you at all what it's like to be godly, or at the very least, of a divine origin. Perhaps you are quite content to be, what the Bible calls: dead. The living-dead, of course. A zombie.

Let us examine the biblical proposition.

The Bible never claims that anyone can ever become God. This position has been filled before time began. It will be there after the time runs out. No one ever managed to define God. According to Spinoza, it can't be done.[153] Some came close. I like: "God is what the opposites have in common." Or: "God is That which Is." The Old Testament uses the famous tetragrammaton YHWE, i.e.: Yahveh or Yahweh. This abbreviation was known to the Hebrews as the Incommunicable Name of God, and, since the name is so sacred, they pronounced it Elohim. The nearest we can come to the

---

[153] Baruch Spinoza (1632-77) held that: "to define God is to deny God", i.e.: one cannot place limitations on that which is infinite.

meaning of YHWH is The Existing One, the Eternal One, Self-Existent. Being more analytical, the letters *Yod*, *Hé*, *Wau*, and *Hé* represent the (universal) masculine and feminine principles, or that which lies at the origin of all.

Since the ancient days, the Bible has been rewritten many times.[154] Suffice to say that at least some of the scribes, entrusted with the arduous task of rewriting by hand the ancient manuscripts, must have suffered from a considerable lack of divine inspiration. They managed to translate the various names of God as El, Elah, Elohim, Eloah, Jehovah, Jah, Lord, Lord God, to mention but a few. But we do not have to worry. With one exception, none of the above deal with our own potential of becoming gods.

Please note, gods with a very small 'g'.

But God cannot be small. God Is.

A paradox?

Not if we are referring to the nature of divinity rather than a Being. Water is water, in a pool or an ocean.

Now, at last, we can get down to the business of becoming gods. First, again, the biblical version. The Bible at no time tells anyone that they are, or are in danger of becoming, God. One cannot become that which already IS. What the Bible does say is that we all are children of the most High. And, if we become aware of this portentous fact, *and* act accordingly, we shall be gods. In Psalm 82 (to which reference is made by all who wish to ascribe to us divine traits), the word *elohim* is translated as "gods". It is that same Hebrew word which is used and translated as "gods" in Genesis 3:5, wherein the scriptures state: "...you shall be *as* gods, knowing good and evil..."

Now at least we know that being god-like is knowing good and evil.

---

[154] H.P. Blavatsky in ISIS UNVEILED examines extensively the origins of the Old Testament.

This may or may not be such a good thing. By relegating us to a mental state of judgement, we are told that we can only be (as) gods in a dualistic state of consciousness, i.e.: in a material-emotional-mental world. Since true divinity (being One) is beyond duality, we can at least rest assured that we are in no danger of ever having to enter into direct competition with God. Just as well, for I strongly suspect, it might prove a loosing proposition.

So who are these gods who will, ultimately, populate this earth? Some divine beings of the future? If the scriptures are right, and apparently they cannot be broken[155], I do hope the Christians accept the concept of reincarnation. If not, they, in order to preserve the integrity of the scriptures, would have to become gods in this, their present life. Good luck. So little time...
We would better start straight away.
The first step is to define what we mean by god-like. Unless we can define what we mean by this term, it can hardly become the object of your or mine contemplation. So – how does a god act? A master is a man, or woman, who acts like a master. A god is a man/woman who acts like a god. Conversely, our actions are the fruit of what we are.[156] It may be wise to make a list of our (future) divine traits. We must decide what sort of gods we wish to be. Regrettably, there is a catch. According to the very same scriptures, if we make the *right* choices, we will be reviled by most.[157] In other words, if George[158] decides to be a god-in-waiting, then he'll soon find that no one will appreciate his efforts. Everyone will misunderstand him. He will be told that he's con-

---

[155] John 10:35
[156] Matthew 7:16
[157] Matthew 5:11 For "my sake" means for all that I stand for, i.e.: for the 'things of the spirit'.
[158] You are free to substitute your name for George.

ceited, self-centred, all-knowing, with an altogether inflated ego.

But that's only if he makes the *right* choices!

In fact, George is not conceited, but is developing incorruptible faith in the omnipotence of his Higher Self. He learned not to rely on his ego, knowing it to be a manifestation of a transient universe. Instead, he leans on the aspect of his being which he believes to be his indestructible essence. Next, George is dubbed self-centred. Now that's very true, providing we spell Self with a capital "S". That which to others is, at best, a supposition, to George is the only True Reality. Next, George is accused of sounding like a know-it-all. That is also true, though, again, it carries a completely different meaning. As far as his ego is concerned, George is deeply convinced that he knows nothing. Less every day. Socrates reached the very same conclusion some two-and-a-half thousand years ago. George does believe, however, in the omniscience of his Higher Self.

Poor George. He has still other problems!

Apparently, his repeated assurances that he does not have the slightest desire to impose his belief system on any other person invariably falls on deaf ears. To George, the spiritual realm is a Realm of *absolute freedom*. How could he possibly want to impose his will or beliefs on others? His willingness to share his reality is misinterpreted as an imposition of such. George firmly believes in the utter uniqueness of every blade of grass. "Can people be any less?" He asked me.

George believes all that. All he must do now is to let his beliefs grow into knowledge, into practice. Details, details... he likes to say with a very broad smile. But George is not worried. He believes that gods are immortal.

Regardless of what people say.

***

34

VENGEANCE

There are a number of agencies pursuing war criminals. The winning side invariably extracts vengeance from the losing one. With the exception of Canada in recent months, few, if ever, pursue the crimes of those on the winning side.

There are organizations and individuals that specialize in pursuing near ninety-year-old Nazis, in order to inflict vengeance on them. As if the human mind was capable of inventing punishment for someone that tortured and/or murdered thousands.

And then there are journalists, brave men and women, risking their lives (as well as welfare of their families), in the pursuit of drug-lords, dealers, distributors of narcotics. Some, (also journalists – the job is too dangerous for politicians) attempt to extract vengeance from the tobacco companies whose product is equally as deadly. Those few who pursue this latter group, find the tobacco-barons as formidable opponents as any other drug-lords. Fewer still, attempt to inflict vengeance the magnates of pharmaceutical companies whose vastly overpriced concoctions are known to destroy the lives of many.[159]

And finally... the Holy See indulges in its own inimitable version of unholy vengeance. The church, seemingly unaware of the dictates of the Scriptures, attempts to extract retribution even beyond the temporal limitations. The church fathers cast anathema on those who disagree with them.[160]

Ah, vengeance is sweet – and yet....

"Vengeance is mine; I will repay, saith the Lord".[161] This biblical statement alone should prohibit Christians from seeking vengeance. Does it?

"Why should the Lord have all the fun?" asks the holier-than-thou, just itching to get even. "Why can't I be the one who metes out justice, punishment, retribution."

"Give me vengeance or give me death!" cry the noble soldiers marching into a hail of bullets. Doesn't the Lord know what satisfaction it gives? What sweet, intoxicating feeling it is to do-unto-others as one would never have anyone do-unto-oneself? ...only in revenge, of course. We don't kill in cold blood. We murder only in vengeance. We are too civilized to do so otherwise.

Aren't we? Are we?

"To me belongeth vengeance, and recompense..."[162] This quotation absolves all the adherents to the Judaic tradition from the necessity of seeking vengeance over the Nazis. It further relieves them from the obligation of dynamiting and running bulldozers over the homes of their neighbours. It was Moses who admonished the Hebrews to *love* their neighbour,

---

[159] The word pharmaceutical comes from Greek *pharmakon* meaning poison or medicine.
[160] Latin, from Greek anathema = anything devoted to evil, like the Roman Catholic church excommunication which, in some peoples' minds, is tantamount to eternal damnation.
[161] Romans 13:19
[162] Deuteronomy 32:35

VENGENCE

not to exact vengeance.[163] And if we quarrel with the definition of the word "neighbour" – don't the Palestinians claim to be, equally, the children of Abraham?

And it's all so ludicrous!
Even if we choose to ignore the Jewish and the Christian ethic, (and it is abundantly clear that, *en masse*, we do), there is a superb revelation given us by the sages of the East. It is called Karma. The word Karma means many things to many people, but in the context of vengeance, it carries a particularly comforting meaning. It is the law of balance. It means that a state of balance shall be restored here, on earth, regardless whether anyone of us chooses to believe in this law or not. What goes up must come down. It's really that simple. It is the law that sets the action and reaction on an automatic cycle. No amount of supplicatory prayer at the Wailing Wall in Jerusalem, or at the gates of Vatican, or at the great mosque – the Haram, shall or can, alter its immutable mandate[164]. The Christian ethic echoes its rigor: Whatsoever *a man soweth... so shall he also reap.*[165] Or *...all they that take the sword* (hatred, anathema, bulldozer, etc.) *shall perish with the sword.*[166] This is the law of Karma. Inviolable and immutable.

Supposing a man borrows money from me and leaves the country. Supposing I shall never be able to trace his steps (to extract vengeance). Knowing the law of Karma, I need not worry, for two reasons. One, the man who thinks that he's

---

[163] Leviticus 19:18

[164] This or any other law, compare Luke 16:17: "And it is easier for heaven and earth to pass, than one tittle of the law to fail". [The great mosque, the Haram, encloses the Kaaba (chief goal of Moslem pilgrimages) is in Mecca].

[165] compare Galatians 6:7

[166] Matthew 26:52 Compare Genesis 9:6: Whoso sheddeth man's blood, by man shall his blood be shed... All such quotations attest to man's early knowledge of the law of Karma.

outwitted me has not done so. Sooner or later, he shall be called upon to repay not only the amount he failed to return, but also suffer all the unpleasantness his behaviour may have caused me. But that's not all. I, the "injured party" shall not be injured at all. How is this possible? Simple. Everything you or I possess, be they physical possessions or mental attributes, are, in reality, states of consciousness. If the given amount of money was "truly mine", i.e.: I have earned it, then anyone's failure to honour the debt will in no way shortchange me. The exact amount, plus the accrued "interest", shall be returned to me. From whatever source.

How do I know? It happened to me. More than once!

Karma is but one of the laws governing the universe. The knowledge enshrined in the Vedas, the Bhagavad Gita, in the Mysteries of the Ancient Egyptians, Chaldeans, Assyrians, Chinese, Greeks, Essenes, Hebrews and the Scriptures of countless others, is not a religious dissertation to be exploited for the purpose of subjugating naîve people, but a conglomerate of priceless textbooks exuding golden wisdom, affirming universal laws. Pretending they don't exist in no way protects us from every ounce of "retribution" being exacted from our bank accounts, our emotional and/or mental attachments. In other words, ignorance of law is no excuse for breaking it. Whether we accept the existence of the law of Karma, (or any other universal law), we still live under its Damoclesian blade.

It bears repeating – the world is set "on automatic".

If we choose to live in this universe, we must obey its laws. Once we fathom the wisdom of the law of Karma, vengeance doesn't make any sense. Not because we no longer care about justice not being done without our intervention, but because the balance will be restored *regardless* of our intervention.

So what should we do? Sit back and watch the world unfold? I could think of worse things to do, but – no such luck! We each have a role to play, a destiny to fulfil. Discovering what is that role is part of the fun. Fulfilling it – immensely greater. But no role calls for sitting in judgement over other, less fortunate people, who, at their present level of evolution, are not yet able to rise to our dubious heights. Or sink to the depth of our prideful depravity.

Or simply – to love their neighbour.

***

970203

There is no greater obstacle to God than time.

Meister Eckhart
(1260–1327)

I am baffled by the way sophisticated theologians who know Adam and Eve never existed still keep talking about it.

Richard Dawkins

[Ed. Note. Ignorance is not always bliss. Adam symbolizes the conscious mind, Eve the subconscious.]

*...'tis in ourselves that we are thus or thus.
Our bodies are our gardens,
to the which our wills are gardeners;
so that if we will plant nettles, or sow lettuce,
set hyssop and weed up thyme, supply it with one gender of
herbs, or district it with many,
either to have it sterile with idleness,
or manured with industry, why, the power
and corrigible authority of this lies in or wills.*

William Shakespeare
[OTHELLO]
Act I, scene III.

35

PURPOSE

"**To be, or not to be.**" The bard suggests we have a choice! For the sake of an argument, let us opt for the state of being. Perhaps there is a purpose to our life. Perhaps there is a purpose to our inquiry. But there is a condition. If I am "to be", I want to be happy. Why bother to be, otherwise? He who wishes to suffer will hardly ponder such questions. But you and I have made our decision. We have established our purpose.

"To live happily, is the desire of all men, ...but their minds are blinded to a clear vision of just what it is that makes life happy;" wrote Lucius Seneca some 2000 years ago.[167] The Epicureans, followed by the Stoics, searched intensively for the elixir of happiness. Some claimed to have it almost in their grasp. Some were branded heretics for daring to pursue pleasure. But in all cases, men felt obliged to justify not only their desire but even the outcome of their pursuit. Yet none seem to have made it. Not altogether. The error lay in man's confusing the effect, with the cause. The Hedonists assumed pleasure to be the purpose of their search, whereas in fact, the state of bliss is no more than a result.

What then – of purpose?

Let us examine this troublesome word. It is derived from Latin: *Proponere*, to place before (*pro* – before, *ponere* – to place). Thus, if we long to be happy, i.e. if we prefer

---

[167] Lucius Anneus Seneca (4 B.C.-65 A.D.), playwright, author and statesmen. From his essay ON THE HAPPY LIFE.

pleasure to pain, we must define our purpose. We must define that which precedes, and results in, this desirable condition. Poets, philosophers, saints and saviours, all tried to answer this apparent enigma. Some ancients identified the purpose as that which precedes an action. "I have purposed it, I will also do it", avers Isaiah.[168] In the prophet's case the effect of the cause shall be action. But surely, action, *per se*, does not guarantee a beatific condition. Action can, in turn, assure a result; it can become a precipitant of wealth, fame, the world. But, "for what is a man profited, if he shall gain the whole world, and lose his own soul?"[169] Can one be happy devoid of one's soul? The plot thickens... And here's the rub, as Shakespeare would justly point out. If the loss of our soul is a concomitant to the conquest of the world, wherefore do we go from here?

Back to the young prince's question: "To be or not to be?"

What is this state of being? Is he who loses his soul no longer? Or is soul that which defines our state of being. Perhaps "to be," means to be aware of one's own existence. I think, therefore I am?[170] What if I don't think? Do I cease to be? As what? As an ephemeral bunch of atoms which we breathe in and breathe out in great abundance with every longing sigh? Are we the dust which in no way differs from that upon which we tread daily? Perhaps we are a "mind"... which also ceases to be, the moment our "soul" leaves our hapless body.

No. The mind too is too transient.

It seems more and more that the necessary ingredient of happiness is a condition of being which is not subject to the

---

[168] Isaiah 46:11

[169] Matthew 16:26

[170] René Descartes (1596-1650) "Discourse on the Method of Rightly Conducting the Reason."

slings and arrows of outrageous fortune.[171] What if our purpose is to identify within us, within the essence of our being, that which is free, independent, beyond the influences of external conditions... Would that not offer us a taste of this elusive elixir of happiness?

To be or not to be...

A man who has no purpose – has no aim in life. A ship without a rudder.

Once again, to find happiness, which is a result – not the cause for our search, we must define our purpose. It is a long search. Yet when we gather the conclusions of the great minds, of the great sages of the human condition, there is one consistent statement which rings true in all their teachings: Know *thyself*. Find out what, but more so, *who* you are. This is the underlying purpose of *all* that follows. Ultimately, after many a lifetime, we discover that we are immortal. That no power on earth can in anyway do us mischief. That the real Self cannot be broken or stolen, drowned or otherwise injured in anyway whatever. Once we discover this mystery, we are a long, long way towards a blissful state of being.

The search for Truth is not for the timid. The searcher will navigate his ship against most arduous currents. Yet only the truth can set us free from the wiles, illusions, of this taxing kindergarten. Finally, the tests are over. Finally, after aeons of existence, we are free to enjoy all we have ever dreamed of. The sky is the limit. No! There are no more limits! We can reach for the moon. (Some did and they made it!) We are well on the way to taking charge of our kingdom. Our heritage? The world. Though it was *not* the world we were seeking. What we sought was, simply, the nature of our being.

No one shall ever again fool us that we must "die" to

---

[171] W. Shakespeare: As is the quotation on first page: Hamlet's monologue (see below).

"go" to heaven. Heaven, we know now, is a state of being; and happiness ensues from the knowledge of Truth. We've reached our home. HERE AND NOW. They who don't find it while alive and kicking, what chance have they lying dead and buried?

We can now tell the fair prince of Denmark that we have chosen "being". Now that we know who we are, and wherefore...

To be, and to be happy. Was there ever a question?

***

970204

To be, or not to be: that is the question:
Whether 'tis nobler in the mind to suffer
The slings and arrows of outrageous fortune,
Or to take arms against a sea of troubles,
And by opposing end them?
To die: to sleep;
No more;
and by a sleep to say we end
The heart-ache and the thousand natural shocks
The flesh is heir to, 'tis a consummation
Devoutly to be wish'd.

William Shakespeare
HAMLET
[Act III, Sc.I]

36

GENESIS

In my essay on CREATIVITY I attempted to define the interrelationship between the creator, creating and the created. Here I wish to review the creative process itself, with particular reference to the biblical model as illustrated in the first chapter of Genesis.[172] Great many people are still under an illusion that Genesis describes the "God's" idea as to how the universe, or at the very least the earth, had been created. Apparently it all happened in just seven days. God, according to those people, ignored His own laws, set time aside by a few billion years, decided that evolution is hereby cancelled, and proceeded to perform his conjuring tricks, not the least of which was extracting Eve from Adam's rib. Recently, even the Vatican granted us permission to believe in evolution – if we so wish. We don't have to, but we may.

One up for Galileo!

So what is the first chapter of Genesis all about? If not about the creation of the world then what? Surely God did have something to do with it all.

The answer will differ with the meaning of the word God. There are no two people who hold the same Truth sacred when it comes to the conceptualization of the Creative force. The latest, perhaps the most propitious, belongs to Deepak Chopra, who describes the Infinite Source as the Field of Infinite Possibilities. Why not? After all, it is we who decide What or Who it is that we choose to believe in. And the days of an ancient Man floating among the clouds in the Sistine Chapel, are over. Hopefully. God is becoming less

---

[172] Actually the first chapter plus first 3 verses of chapter two. The biblical subdivisions have often little to do with subject matter.

and less anthropomorphic. Less and less in our image and likeness.

Back to Genesis.
The first chapter is nothing more than a symbolic description of a creative process. Not of earth, not of the world, but of the Process. Nothing ever becomes manifest in the physical universe unless it went through the Process of Creation. I capitalize the words because whatever we define as Divinity is an integral, inseparable part of this activity. Let's see the Bible.

***

In the beginning God created the heaven and the earth. (Genesis 1:1)
Two important items of information are hidden in the very first verse. One, God is always at the beginning of everything, and two, in order for anything to become manifest, to "happen", we need to initiate the concept of duality. In "heaven", every idea is in its potential state. On earth, it is concretized. Thus, the two states of consciousness: the spiritual (heaven) and the non-spiritual (earth).[173] Before anything at all can happen this concept must be accepted. It is imperative to remember that there is no duality in the spiritual realm; nor, by definition, is there any "matter". To successfully convert a (spiritual) Idea into concrete (material) forms we must follow the instructions closely.

And the earth was without form, and void; and darkness

---

[173] Since writing this essay, I've suggested that matter is spirit at greatly reduced vibrations. Since God, or Spirit is omnipresent, it is logical to assume that matter is also a manifestation of Sprit in a different form. This in no way challenges the validity of the essay on Genesis (Nov.'99).

was upon the face of the deep. And the spirit of God moved upon the waters. (ibid., verse 2)

Obviously, the earth (matter) was without form; it was void, i.e. it wasn't there! It was only a *potential* form. It was an idea. The darkness always represents the absence of Light, and Light always stands for knowledge. We are dealing here, as practically everywhere in the Bible, with symbols. Since the Bible concerns itself exclusively with spiritual matters, the knowledge it refers to is Divine knowledge. Next, the *face* symbolizes the power of recognition. At this stage there is nothing to recognize. The *waters* symbolize the thought-stream. So we now have an Idea, an incredible potential (the deep), yet without any knowledge what to do with it! The Spirit is attempting to spiritualize the thought-stream. The uncoordinated thoughts are the original building blocks of the universe, and thus of absolutely anything within the universe. They are what atoms were before they became atoms. They could be regarded as quanta of energy and information not yet organized into patterns.

And God said. Let there be light; and there was light. (ibid., verse 3)

As stated above, light is the source of all knowledge. An illuminated person is a knowledgeable person. To put ideas into concrete forms we need knowledge.

And God called the light Day, and the darkness he called Night. (ibid., verse 5)

This is a fascinating piece of instruction. We recognize the day as time between sunrise and sunset. The Hebrew did the opposite. The Hebrew *day started at sunset.* In order for an Idea to take root, we must *not* try to think about it but... sleep! The greatest ideas anyone ever had did not take seed in the scientists' labs, but at night. We are reminded here about the true source of ideas, and the true "developer" of such. The nearest we get to participate is through our unconscious. So much for our egos!

And God said, Let there be a firmament in the midst of the waters, and let it divide the waters from the waters. (ibid., verse 6)

I love the King James Version of the Bible. But when poetry and accuracy compete for attention, poetry wins! The Hebrew word *raqia*, translated as "firmament", in fact means *expanse* or *expansion*. What we are told here is that we must go through the process of sifting our thoughts into the relevant and the irrelevant. As the Idea grows, our thought processes must be concentrated. We must divide them from other thoughts. If we are to develop an idea, we cannot be scatterbrains. The great thinkers, inventors, artists, invariably demonstrate fantastic powers of concentration. The ancients knew that!

The following verse deals with the same subject. It is interesting (verse 8), that *God called the firmament Heaven.* It suggests that the process of expansion of ideas is still a "divine" process, i.e. it must take place before the idea enters our conscious mind. We love saying that *we* have a marvelous idea. It seems, if the idea is any good, it originated way above the "we" or the "I" concepts. Our egos take another beating...

And God said, Let the waters under the heaven be gathered together unto one place, and let the dry land appear: (ibid., verse 9)

We made it. Finally dry land. When we gather together our thoughts (waters), under the heaven, i.e. in our conscious mind, a manifestation takes place. Emmet Fox, the superb exponent of the spiritual interpretation of the Bible, called this a Demonstration. If we follow the process accurately, if we let "God" do His work (mostly when we sleep), if we are humble enough to let our thoughts be gathered at our unconscious level *before* we take active part in the process, we end up with a demonstration. If we are so pigheaded as to think that we, ourselves, with the use of 5% of our brains, can develop an original idea, well.... Good luck. It would be a first!

The rest of the creative process described in Genesis shows us how not to rush an idea. How to keep checking, at every stage, if the idea is "good". This simply means that if our ego takes over, we might channel the idea for our own ends, for our personal gain or advantage. God, whatever we mean by this Concept, is ONE. IT (or He) is not concerned with our puny egos but with All. As we grow in Light, in Divine Knowledge, our interests begin to reflect that which can benefit the largest number. R. Buckminster Fuller wrote that in 1927 (at the age of 32), he committed all his productivity potential toward dealing only with our whole planet. He continued: "This decision was not taken on a recklessly altruistic do-gooder basis, but in response to the fact that my Chronofile clearly demonstrated that in my first 32 years of life I had been positively effective in producing life-advantage wealth... ...only when I was doing so entirely for others and not for myself."[174]

Genesis, so aptly named, is not about the "birth" of the world. It is about the birth of an IDEA. (The world, of course, is rather a divine idea!) All ideas are always of divine origin. Real, original ideas. Not those spawned by our plagiarizing egos. In allowing ideas to be developed through our souls, minds, states of consciousness, we partake in a divine act. For some ephemeral instants, we are gods!

***
970210

---

[174] Fuller, R.Buckminster CRITICAL PATH [St. Martin's Press] pg. 124-5. Mr. Fuller gained renown as an inventor in many fields and became known as "the planet's friendly genius".

*"It is almost a miracle that modern teaching
methods have not strangled
the holy curiosity of inquiry;
for what this delicate little plant needs more than
anything, besides stimulation, is freedom."*

Albert Einstein

37

THE MESSAGE
&
THE MESSENGER

Mozart is dead. So are Beethoven, Schubert, and Chopin. So are Socrates, Plato, Dante and Shakespeare. So are Krishna, Moses, Lao-tse, Buddha, Zoroaster and Jesus of Nazareth. They are all dead. Their Messages – live on. Therein the true immortality of the messengers. Therein their glory. Therein their perpetual gifts to humanity. It is for their Messages that we offer them honour. Our admiration. Our love.

There is an Ocean of Infinite Potential. A priceless Source, an inexhaustible Spring of Life, of Truth, of Beauty, ready to be discovered, ready to be brought out into the open. It is there, waiting, eternally available to share Its bounty. Within Its realm await the Messages. The priceless gifts. We, you and I, need the messengers to bring them to us. We need the great messengers to open their hearts, their eyes, their ears. We, at our stage of evolution, don't as yet know how to listen, to see. We often think we know, but this presumption is little more than an illusion fostered by our pride. It is this illusion which also stops us from searching for the Truth. None are so blind as those who have eyes and cannot see. Well, we can't. Not yet. We still need the messengers.

But let us never confuse the letter with the postmen.

The Infinite Source, God if you like, has no desire to remain hidden. No scriptures ever claimed that. "For nothing is secret, that shall not be made manifest; neither anything hid, that shall not be known..."[175]. All Messages are available to all who would listen. What gets in the way is our conditioning. The knowledge we have already acquired is a jealous knowledge. It refuses to be pushed aside to make room for the new. We tend to get caught in our little ruts. We are weighed down by our mores and morals, by our precious customs and traditions, by that which keeps us apart – like culture, education, heritage. We are set in our petty ways.

I heard is said that no mathematical discovery had been made by anyone over the age of 26. Apparently there are neuro-connectors which, through non-use, atrophy. Don't use it – loose it. It also applies to our brains. The wisdom of the years helps us to interpret what is, not to introduce and accept new concepts. For the *new* we need youth. Not necessarily "chronological" youth, but a youthful state of consciousness. New concepts call on us to wipe the slate clean and to be born anew. Paul, the apostle, a messenger, said that he dies daily.[176] Daily! He dies to all his accumulated knowledge in order to make room for the new. To become rejuvenated. To delve deeper into the Ocean of Truth. Paul found it necessary. Do we? Do we even want to? Or would we rather die of boredom than risk loosing what is safe, comfortable? It seems that it is not the Truth that we love, but the emotional security that our acquired beliefs provide.

Let us beware. Such safety is an illusion. It is brittle.

---

[175] Luke 8:17. Compare Matthew 10:26
[176] 1 Corinthians 15:31

Deceiving.

"I make all things new", said a young teacher from Nazareth[177]. *All* things. A complete renewal. Strange. He, like Paul, chose to renew all, but those who claim to follow in their footsteps cling to the past. This is what happens when we cling assiduously to the robe of the messenger while ignoring his message. "Freedom comes when the mind experiences without tradition," said Krishnamurti, a recent messenger.[178] Never mind if we don't know who is Krishnamurti. But can we recognize his Message?

An even more modern teacher, Deepak Chopra, talks of shelf-life of ideas.[179] We are all conversant with this concept. It simply defines the length of time that a stored item remains usable. Our foodstuffs spoil within days, weeks at best. Our furniture wears out in a few years. Our cars, utensil, items of everyday use, have even shorter span of usefulness. Even our bodies deteriorate with time. But ideas?

Mozart's music is a fresh today, as it was on the day that the young messenger transferred it to paper. The ideas of Socrates ring true today, thanks to Plato whose own message survived 23 centuries. But the longest shelf-life, surely, belongs to the Messages of the great avatars. The Vedas are so old we lost track of the messengers who brought them.[180] Other great envoys negated their own egos to become pure instruments for the transference of ideas from the Infinite Source to our unwilling ears. Why unwilling? Don't we judge their shelf-life by the amount of dust they gather? And yet, many an envoy died young, castigated, rejected by their own people. All for the sake of the Message.

---

[177] Revelation 21:5
[178] Jayakar, Pupul KRISHNAMURTI, A Biography (Harper & Raw)
[179] Chopra, Deepak AGELESS BODY, TIMELESS MIND
[180] The Rig-Veda, Yajur-Veda, Sama-Veda and others are the Sanskrit scriptures of Hinduism

The next time we hear real music, let us listen for the celestial overtones. The Music of the Spheres. And when we listen to a humble speaker, let us not question his worldly credentials, lest we might miss his Message. He knows he is but an instrument. A postman delivering an immortal Message. If we listen hard, we just might extend even our own existence. By attrition – a sort of rubbing off.

By the power within the Message.

But most of all let us try to hear the message before it becomes perverted. Rather than listening to "updated" music, philosophies or spiritual Messages twisted beyond recognition, let us try to get as close as we can to the Source. Some of It still lingers within the yellow pages of old manuscripts, but mostly the Source is within us. To hear It, we must become very still – and learn to listen.

We, if we only realize it, are the true keepers of the enduring Message.

Deep within.

If we only realize it.

***

970212

*And he said unto them,
"How is it that ye do not understand?"*

Mark 8:21

38

NECESSITIES

There are two fundamental modes of existence. Material or physical and spiritual or metaphysical.[181] The physical mode, we, humans, share with all other animals. This level of existence concerns itself with all that we regard as necessities of racial, national, group and/or individual physical survival. It deals with propagation, nourishment, and protection of our families, groups, of our common ways of life. Until recently, the tasks within this *modus vivendi* held a sharp demarcation between the male and the female responsibilities. The female was almost solely responsible for the propagation, leaving the male to tend to the nourishment and protection aspects. It is characteristic of this mode of consciousness that very often the common good takes precedence over the good of an individual.

Obviously, in this context, the good of the species, at least in theory, must prevail. This particular mindset, or genetic conditioning, is common to all animals who wish to protect their chances of survival by congregating in herds, flocks, droves, prides, gaggles, swarms, casts, sects, villages, cities or nations. The purpose of any of these congregations is

---

[181] It is ironic that the word meta-physical literally means "after physics", whereas the "spiritual" is understood to precede the physical manifestation, not follow it.

to assure communal survival of a particular faction, or specie, usually at the expense of another group. The degeneration of this mindset, or mentality, is self evident in the creation of subgroups, such as armies, hosts, legions, mobs and rabble, which far from protecting the species, go a long way towards its extermination. Perhaps this form of mentality senses, at some primordial level, that ultimately, everything physical meets its end. It dies.

The second mode of existence, the spiritual, is almost exactly the opposite.

It has nothing to do with any of the above, though physical survival is of some, if negligible, consequence. In a way, "spiritual survival" is an oxymoron. That, which is of spirit, cannot die. By definition. The threats of death and damnation popular in authoritarian i.e.: orthodox religions likewise cannot have anything to do with spiritual reality. That, which is material will, in time, irrevocably be transferred to a different form of energy or matter. That which is spiritual is static. It never changes. It is eternal.

All ancient scriptures teach the transcendence of matter.

We find it in the ancient Veda, the Tao-teh-king[182], the four noble truths and the eightfold path of Buddha, the teaching of Yeshûa of Nazareth who became known to us as Jesus. Yet the purpose of all these seemingly esoteric advocates has never been how to escape life. The purpose of all great teachers had been how to enhance our sojourn on this earth. How to avoid pain. How to heighten our pleasure, our delight, our appreciation of the world around us. No matter how illusory. To them the physical world was not an intransigent solid matter, but a malleable, flexible reality, ever ready to flow into

---

[182] The philosophy of Taoism is ascribed to Lao-tse. Originally he taught the desirability of escape from the illusion of desire through mystical contemplation. Some scholars place Lao-tse's birth as early as 604 B.C.

new forms, new shapes, to enhance our lives. None of the great teachers taught us how to die. They taught us how to live. Here and now.

Years after their death others came and twisted their teaching beyond recognition. Perhaps not on purpose. To anyone unaware of his or her spiritual nature, the original teaching is incomprehensible. One thousand years after Laotse's death, his followers adopted many gods and formed monastic orders. The followers of Buddha did not wait so long. His "middle path" once more searched for extremes, though retained a relatively greater contact with the original teaching. Perhaps that is why there are fewer crimes committed by Buddhists than by the adherents of any other religion. But talking of crimes, the greatest such were, and continue to be, committed against the teaching of Jesus. His prolific examples of a happy existence, which he called heaven, were twisted beyond recognition. Although the essence of his philosophy is still readily available in the Gospels, few of his "followers" ever take the trouble to read, let alone study, the concise statements attributed to him. Most of us prefer to listen to countless, perhaps well meaning, sacerdotal do-gooders, feeding us their incomprehensible interpretations.

But if so, what is "spiritual" life? How does it differ from the material, physical, animalistic, transient existence?

It differs in one thing only. It differs in the State of Consciousness. There are many, mostly religious people, who think of themselves as nice men and women, who, through the beneficence of a great, unknown Being have been granted a soul. Few, if any, can define at all precisely what do they mean by this "soul", but they say they "have" one. Apparently, when they die, their "soul" shall take an express journey to either hell or heaven. Or a rerun to a cleansing laboratory known to them as purgatory. These people are often very preoccupied with death. Their eternity hangs on it.

And then there is a tiny fraction of the human race that doesn't believe they possess a soul. They believe, many know beyond a shadow of doubt, that they ARE Soul. Or more precisely, each is a singular, unique individualization of Soul. They are minute sparks of the Eternal Flame endowed with self-awareness. They are the indivisible parts of the integral ONE. They know they are spiritual beings, spending a brief, fleeting sojourn on earth, encased in a retinue of atoms moulded into biological constructs, all for the purpose of learning. They are here learning to become conscious participators in the creative process of Life. Many have just taken their first tentative steps on this exhilarating journey, and already they seem drank with the euphoria, with the elixir of immortality. They do not dwell on the necessities, which seem to preoccupy other states of consciousness. Yet, to their constant amazement, as they seek to fathom the mysteries of the Kingdom, all other necessities are furnished for them. Automatically.

Didn't someone once say that this very thing would happen? He must have. He had so many other incredible ideas... [183]

***

970213

---

[183] Matthew 6:33, Luke 12:31; also 1 Kings 3:13, Psalm 37:25, et al..

39

QUESTIONS

Who amongst us would tell lions how to run their pride, buffaloes – how to control their herd, ants – how to construct an anthills? The most learned men or women have not the slightest idea what genetic technology are dolphins using in their communications. Which one of us can navigate an airplane from Canada to Latin America, regardless of weather, without the use of a single chart or a radio contact? A butterfly can. So can many a bird. We can't.

Ah, but look at our medical advances! Look at our scientific progress in surgery, artificial joints, and technologically advanced prosthesis. But can we re-grow our limbs (or tail)? A reptile can. (A flatworm can re-grow a lot more than that.) But look at the vaccines we invented! Have we? A monkey developed an immune system to overcome the AIDS virus. How come we haven't? A lowly bug, a virus, can outwit armies of scientists having at their disposal millions in taxpayers' money. And what of flesh eating bacteria? Why can't we eat them, instead? And what of bacteria becoming immune to our treasured antibiotics. How come we are not becoming immune to them?

"Be fruitful, and multiply, and replenish the earth, and subdue it.... and have dominion over every living thing that moveth upon the earth".[184] Except over what you cannot kill or maim, or otherwise render harmless. But keep trying. One day you might just clear the earth of just about everything that moveth. Especially if it doesn't fight back. Like the stupid bacteria.

---

[184] Genesis 1:28

Or perhaps we shouldn't take the Bible quite so literally?

We, most of us, appear to feel superior to our environment. We look down at other forms of life. We created religions that affirm that we are masters of the earth. We are gods, drunk with power! We even developed capability to create a nuclear winter. Well... so have a thousand volcanoes. So has anyone of a thousand asteroids, which a wondering comet can nudge from its orbit towards our backyard. The resulting dust-cloud would prohibit sunrays from reaching the earth. Photosynthetic process would stop. With it – our life. Masters indeed!

A single asteroid, a single volcanic explosion.... A "nuclear" winter without a single atomic bomb exploded. Accidents will happen. Like a rose or an orchid. Are they not also accidents of nature? Like the starlit sky, the majesty of Rocky Mountains, the indomitable fury of a raging ocean, dreamy serenity of a summer's twilight... All accidents, illusions?

Vanity of vanities... 'tis all vanity.

Or accidents.

Perhaps, after all, we too are part of nature. Perhaps we are no more than vain hirelings of whoever pulls our strings? An Alien or a Spirit? And if we were unable to tell a virus, an insect, fish, bird, reptile or mammal how to run his or her life, why would anyone tell us how to run our ephemeral existence? Isn't there an infinitely greater chasm between such an Alien or Spirit, or Master Puppeteer and us – than between a microscopic virus and us humans? A virus and we are made up of the very same atoms, the same decaying biological structures. But Spirit?

An Alien?

If Spirit be the rider, then we're a pesky stallion. If

Spirit be reality, then we – transient illusion. Spirit – profuse giver, we – takers, exploiters. Spirit – eternal, immortal, we – an evanescent shadow. If Spirit be the Master, then we ever fragmented puppets rising in rebellion.

Why would such an Alien, such Spirit, bother with such dust as we are?

And yet...

No Alien would ever tell us, humans, how to live, how to organize our puny affairs. Contrary to us, they have too much respect for lower life forms. The most they'd tell us is to give Caesar what's Caesars. To obey the Laws which control *all* nature. They'd say that we do not control our environment, the Laws do – and Laws cannot be broken. That although we are inferior to birds in navigation, to dolphins in communication, though we are much weaker than lions, less agile than monkeys, less deadly than a paltry virus, we have been designed for a specific purpose. That we can discover our particular potential. *But only if we look hard enough.* If we single-mindedly pursue this single objective, this single search.

We think we're endowed with glorious self-awareness; but awareness of what? Of the vortex of atoms swirling all around us? Of illusion? Of maya?

I think, therefore I am. Am I? Am I what?

Or, who am I?

So we think. What folly! Every animal thinks. The processing of information is built into all nature's genes. A DNA double helix is not restricted to humans. And judging by the respect that beast has for its habitat, they think much better then we do. Only we, humans, wallow in our garbage. There is but one Law to which we all seem to ascribe gladly. The Law of survival. Even if we destroy everything in the process.

And we, of flesh and blood, are not even immortal! So

why do we bother?

Now and again an Alien assumes our physical form and reminds us that we have a choice: that we can remain as horses or can become riders. That what we could be cannot be seen nor measured, nor perceived with any of our animal senses. These Avatars are willing to share their knowledge with us, humans. They try to adjust their words to our understanding. In the past they spoke in parables, simple allegories, to penetrate our stubborn mindset, our limitations. Were we *then* still barbarians, five centuries after Buddha, four after Socrates, Plato?

But if today one of them told us that each one of us is an indivisible unit of infinite awareness, held in a vortex of energy and information – would we believe Him? And if such a Man told us that all Reality is but a mode of Being, that there is no hell and no heaven nor any other state nor condition except that perceived by the consciousness we choose to enter – would we believe such "nonsense"? And if He told us that when we dispose of our physical bodies, we do not go anywhere because we, the immortals, live only in the present. Would we believe such an Alien, such Spirit?

Would you?

Or would we offer such a blabbermouth masquerading in human form an extra doze of Valium and send Him on a one-way ticket to nowhere. An Alien would be relatively safe, nowadays. We no longer stone nor crucify heretics. We excommunicate them. We ridicule them, or censor. And if that doesn't work, we might just bury mines under their feet, pretending they're little children.

And ignoring all answers we'd keep asking questions.
Profound questions. Questions that won't be denied.

WHO ARE WE?

***

970224

40

CLONING

Early in March 1997, a Scottish biologist Ian Wilmut extracted DNA from an ewe and inserted it into the ovum removed from another sheep. Then he inserted the thus manipulated ovum into the womb of yet another sheep, where it grew to term.

What a magnificent achievement! After years and years of scientific research and development, after spending of millions and millions of public (or at the very least tax-deductible) money, the illustrious scientist achieved with the DNA what a randy ram had been doing, for millions and millions of years, better, for nothing. Just think, another million years and the humans might get to be as good at it as the rams had been a million years ago.

Whaaaw!!!

The biologist not only deprived the ram of his evolutionarily earned pleasure, but he started a veritable storm of protests, ranging from His Holiness in Vatican, all the way to the president of the U.S. of A. in Washington. At first glance, I fail to see what either of the two gentlemen have to do with a sheep or her, reputedly undignified, impregnation. Bill Clinton, I can understand, might well object to anyone being deprived of his duly earned and deserved sex. But the Pope? Surely, the Vatican does not specialize in sexual matters, so why such brouhaha?

And then I have been enlightened. The official spokesman for the Holy See informed us that every human being has the right to be born in a dignified way. At first I was lost. Surely, it was a sheep that gave birth to the lamb, not a woman. I was still lost. Was anyone proposing that a sheep was to give birth to human babies? Or was it that women should not be forced to give birth to sheep. That, I fully agreed, would be quite undignified. I waited with bated breath for an explanation from the Vatican, but none came. There was a hint, however. The Montreal Gazette reported that human, not to mention sheep, babies should be born in a natural, dignified way. There!

Now we know. Or do we...?

I had the dubious pleasure of witnessing one or two natural birth. The female assumed a convenient posture. She pushed out the baby, bit through the umbilical chord, licked the baby clean of the placenta and – voilà, we have a dignified baby. In case of a human birth, to keep it natural, let us add a few hours of quite excruciating (obviously *not* "inhuman") pain, let us count in the risk to a woman's life, let us add a few thousand dollars in obstetrician's fees, and we have, perhaps though no longer completely natural, but almost as dignified a birth as nature – in Clinton's case, and presumably God – in the case of the Vatican, have prescribed.

But hold it!

Even if the female (she used to be called a woman) was to be impregnated with an ovum enlivened with the DNA from another woman (or man?) rather than with sperm, the method of giving birth would be identical! Same pain for the woman, same placenta all over the baby and sheets, same income to the obstetricians, same, so superbly dignified, arrival in this world. And by the way, I strongly recommend for the sacerdotal advocates of the natural birth to witness at least a few of them, to fully appreciate the indescribable dignity of the occasion. My one satisfaction is that in their next lives they will be incarnated into women's bodies and have a chance to really enjoy the dignity of giving a "natural" birth. I can already hear their screams of agony. Perhaps this is what they mean by purgatory. A sort of cleansing?

For their sake, I hope they are wrong. Ignorance should, perhaps, remain bliss. If the blind must insist on leading the blind, we should help them, rather than let them fall deeper and deeper into the darkness of ignorance.

With utmost respect to all womenfolk, I deferentially suggest that there is nothing dignified, whatever, in giving birth to a baby. It is as animalistic a function as can be assigned to a human body. The miracle of birth does not lie in the expulsion of a mature foetus into the cold reality of the material world, but the incredible joy of providing an opportunity for yet another soul to manifest itself in our midst. Soul, a divine attribute of the Eternal that enables IT to individualize Itself into countless entities, is a miracle in itself. Soul never asks nor commands dignity. This trait is an aspect of the human ego. Ego, in turn, is an attribute of a person. I side with Peter, when he said: "Of a truth, I perceive that God is no respecter of persons".[185]

It seems to me, that the Scottish biologist has a long way to go, before he will free women of a most *undignified* function, so beloved by the Vatican. But, all jesting apart, if I had millions to add to those already spent, to save women from the pain of childbirth, from the long months of discomfort as she carries the foetus, from the invasion of her privacy by all who wish to deprive her *soul* of the freedom of choice... I would gladly donate them. Good luck, Dr. Wilmut. More power to you, and God's speed.

---

[185] Acts 10:34, et al.

And as for Bill Clinton – shame on you, Mr. President. But hear well, my friend; you too will be a woman in your next life. You will climb onto the gynaecological stirrups and spread your legs for inspection. Side by side with the scarlet ex-cardinals. We shall see how dignified you all feel then.

***

970310

For unto us a child is born, unto us a son is given:
and the government shall be upon his shoulder:
and his name shall be called Wonderful,
Counsellor, The mighty God,
The everlasting Father,
The Prince of Peace.

Isaiah 9:6

41

MEN AND WOMEN OF EVERY ILK

Some men are gay, some are sad. And some men are gay regardless which of their emotions attain ascendancy. Conversely, some men and some women appear sad although they are neither gay nor straight. Bisexual? Perhaps. One needs a dictionary to sort out all the nuances. But let's have some straight talk about men who are gay. And about lesbians. And the rest of us. Regardless of our hormonal or emotional predilections.

If we are to assume that Nature controls our nature, and that any deviation from a norm established by Nature (God's creation?) is to be judged as a determinant of the degree of our perversions, then surely, homosexuals, men or women, are no more deviating from the norm than celibate priesthood. The recently published recurring cases of homosexuality within the sacerdotal ranks tend to support this thesis.
Like attracts like.
Alternatively, we might initiate a search for a different reason for hormonal fluctuations among men and women. The pertinent question that comes to mind is: Why would a sexless (or androgynous) soul choose to embody itself within a physical entity endowed with a hormonal imbalance. Has God committed another boo-boo, or is there a reason to this incarceration (or incarnation, if you will).
I say hormonal "imbalance" because I must assume

that Nature has made arrangements with our hormones to assure the perpetuation of the species. Isn't that what Nature is all about? Assuming also that God had a reason to create a dualistic, material universe, I must conclude that there is also a reason for our souls to spend a term encased in a group of marauding atoms we call our bodies. Since gays, lesbians and celibatists are, at least in theory, less apt to contribute to the natural accretion in the human ranks, I must place them in the same category.

So we examine the gays, lesbians, Buddhist monks and the Catholic priests. Possibly, as happy a foursome as one hopes to find, but not necessarily gay. Well, not all of them. But there is a powerful bond between them. The bond of going against the Nature's prime law of self-preservation. In the racial sense, of course. Since I very much doubt that any within the group would willingly agree to have anything in common, we are faced with a considerable dilemma.

To unwrap this enigma, we must examine the most fundamental premise on which our understanding of the world is based. Are we a body (a biological construct) which, after countless millennia of evolution, is capable of establishing a conscious entity we refer to as soul, or are we a soul which chooses, for reasons of its own, to submit itself, as an act of free will, to an embodiment in circumstances most propitious to acquiring certain knowledge.

If we assume the first alternative, then any deviation from the norm whose sole purpose is the propagation of the specie, is an error which should be eliminated, expunged, at all costs, as soon as possible. We, individually, as biological units, can forget all about it. Nature continues to evolve and, in time, through a process of natural selection, it will eliminate such obvious perversions. The units of the species exhibiting hormonal imbalance shall no longer be reproduced. Problem solved, even if it does take another few million years.

The second alternative is much more fascinating. What if we are spiritual entities in search of learning? What if the whole, and the sole, purpose of entering a symbiotic state with a biological entity (the human body with all its embellishments, or appurtenances, such a mind, emotions etc.) is to acquire specific experiences, which will give us a greater understanding of our state of being.

What then?

What if I, a spiritual entity or soul, exhibited in the many states of consciousness which I chose to enter (i.e. my previous incarnations), a certain lack of tolerance. Or, perhaps, some xenophobic tendencies. What if the method of observing, of listening to my elders, more experienced souls, bore no result? What then? What would be the *best possible method* of learning not to do unto others that which I have no wish to be done unto myself? A sort of inverse of the golden rule?

Become the other.

By far the best method. By far the best way to learn, about anything, is to become one with the object of one's contemplation. Some take it upon themselves to lead a celibate life, possibly as the very last chance of exercising free will to overcome the tendency of abusing the members of the opposite sex. The next step might be an incarnation into a body from whose vantage point it might be easier to watch but, perhaps, not touch. There may be a million other reasons, but all to do with learning. No soul inhabiting a gay or lesbian body is supposed to suffer. The days when men believed in gods who handed out carrots and sticks are over. We are, every single one of us, an integral part of an Infinite Whole. We, as souls, submit ourselves to climb the ladder of *spiritual* evolution as fast as we can. And if a celibate, gay or lesbian body will help us to take the next step towards perfection, so be it. It is a blessing, not a scourge. And certainly not a perversion.

We see so many individuals who are desperately afraid of anything that is different; afraid of people who choose to think for themselves; afraid of any deviation from the norm. Those people tend to forget that 'norm' is an abbreviation 'normal', and 'normal' means that which is average. And average is an adjective dealing with a group.

This approach doesn't work for people who think of themselves as souls. A soul is, and always will be, an individualization of the Whole. It is always unique, different from all the others. It was created this way, and this way it shall always remain. People who regard themselves as spiritual entities do not judge others. They know that to be different is to be manifesting a divine trait. They also know that if a particular embodiment is not successful, if the lesson is not learned, then there are many, many 'lives' to come. The lesson shall be repeated *ad nauseam*, until the penny drops. Until we say: aaah... so that is what it was all about! All such people shall forever remain men and women of a different ilk. Be they gay, or celibate, or still manifesting Nature's gift of procreation; of creating biological frameworks which souls can use for gathering experience. Those, amongst us, who are not yet rejoicing in being different, have not yet stepped on a *conscious* journey of spiritual evolution. The normal, the average, all who feel "strength in numbers", are still walking the treadmill. The wheel of Awagawan.

We, the "others", the oddballs, who identify ourselves as souls, tend to become more and more different, as we proceed to the next lesson.

And the next, and the next.

***

970314

42

SEX

"Unto Adam also and to his wife did the Lord God make coats of skins, and clothed them."[186]

And that is when all the problems started. Imagine. Entities devoid of flesh, not to mention skins, zoom and zip around most divine environs. They don't do anything much. There is no need. After all, if you are bodiless, what is there to do? You can't eat or drink, you certainly cannot have sex, let alone – enjoy it. You are an androgynous entity, and there is nothing much to do. Except for zipping around. No wonder Lord God clothed us in skins. It gave us something to do! And a lot of things we shouldn't do also. But, that's the problem with good and evil. The best way we can learn, on earth, wrapped in all that skin, is to compare the results of our actions. Or, if we are a little more advanced, to compare thoughts which result in actions.

So what has all this to do with sex?

That depends on what we do in our skins. If by indulging in sexual relations we learn nothing, then, spiritually

---

[186] *Genesis* 3: 21

speaking, we are wasting our time. If, on the other hand, in the process of exercising our hormones we learn anything at all, then let's enjoy sex for all it's worth. After all, at the animal level, sex is the most creative act we can partake in. If we are lucky, we might be instrumental in reproducing our genes, mixing them with our beloved's, and watch nature develop another skin, into which another spiritual entity might enter, and get some learning done also. We haven't the faintest idea just how nature accomplishes this feat, but we partake in it all the same. We might as well enjoy it. It might be the last bit of carefree pleasure we get until the little darlings leave home... I've heard it said that the first half of our lives is ruined by our parents, the second by our children. It doesn't seem to matter whether you start with the chicken or the egg.

With each new skin we use, we are supposed to get smarter. We are supposed to use the skins, given us by our gracious parents; the guys who nourished us and fed us and clothed us and then screwed us up by imposing their stereotyped ideas on us. After being told a thousand-and-one things which we are *not* supposed to do (in their opinion), we are left with walking the treadmill until the doomsday come. And it will come. Sooner or later an errant asteroid will clear a few trillion stereotyped, pathetic ideas out of our skins, conscious and subconscious, and we shall start all over again.

Unless... we have already learned our lesson.

Back to sex.

It takes two to tango, let alone have sex. The two, tango and sex, are closely related. Usually, one is vertical and the other horizontal. Other than that there is little difference, only tango doesn't usually make anyone pregnant. However, neither would be possible without our skins. Lord God knew exactly what He was doing. And, (this is for all the sacerdotal spoilsports), it is the very same Lord God who decided that sex is supposed to give us pleasure – why else would He had given us skins?

And what if we don't have sex?

What if we all decided to be celibate? Well, as a race, as species, we wouldn't last very long. It would not, of course, affect us as spiritual beings. For a while, we would find another way to be creative. We would paint, play the harp, sculpt, or even write. As souls, we must be creative. That's what Spirit is – a Creative Force. And that's what we were before we got all covered up with skins. A lot of Force and nothing much to do with It. Ergo, the skins. They gave us a focus, a chance to develop. If we, while wrapped in skins, do not practice anything creative, then we are not really alive. We are no more than the skins, than the clothing we use as wrapping.

And so, eventually, once the race of celibatists dies out, we would simply wait until the process of natural selection develops new, perhaps better, skins, wrap them around ourselves, and continue with our creative aspirations. Since we, souls, are immortal, there would be no hurry. In the meantime, we would zip around naked. The great sages to come would call it the Golden Age, and the future prophets would talk of another Garden of Eden. Genesis number two. Alternatively, Lord God would gather some more clay and make us new wrappings. Skins.

It sounds efficient but not much fun. For Lord God, I mean.

Once we get our new skins, however, we are right back where we started – up to our ears in sex. We have little choice. So, as I may have mentioned once or twice before, we might as well enjoy it. If not, we'll get naked again. Furthermore, I truly believe that not to enjoy such a fundamental gift would be really missing the mark. And missing the mark is a sin.[187] However, when applying this pearl of wisdom, we might bear in mind that, at the latest count, there were 57 sexually transmitted diseases. Ouch!

The so-called sex drive, or sex appeal, exemplifies the law of natural attraction; for many, it might well be the only foretaste of the unifying principle they will know (in their present life). Nevertheless, the pleasure associated with sex is derived from this spiritual principle. It is derived from the inherent, if subliminal, desire for two to become one. And while sex may be the only method we have to maintain a good supply of skins, there is nothing to stop us from indulging in all sorts of other creative ventures. The arts and sciences can be just as sexy – with the right frame of mind. Pleasure is a concomitant to *every creative* act.

I am a sexagenarian. I know!

***

970316

The phallus functions is an all-embracing symbol of Hindu religion, but if a street urchin draws one on a wall, it just reflects an interest in his penis.

Carl G. Jung
[188]

---

[187] see my essay on PLEASURE

[188] MAN AND HIS SYMBOLS, *Approaching the Unconscious*, [Dell Publ. Co., Inc.] pg.81

43

PROBLEMS

The wind is howling with a fury of another snowstorm. Some late strugglers are still fighting their way home, doubled over, heads low against the biting wind. Only a madman would be out in such weather, if he didn't have to. I left the office a little early. I feel contented. A crystal decanter of rich Cockburn's Porto shimmers deep, full-bodied hues, in front of a crackling fire. I have no problems. I'll just stretch my legs, perhaps listen to some Vivaldi, escape the wintry reality with a good novel, and forget the whistling gale. I've earned my rest. Isn't life beautiful?

The telephone rings.

Five minutes later, I don my snowshoes, grab a tennis racked and drive, walk, fight my way through the blizzard to the local indoor tennis club. I slug it out with my friends for two long hours. Then I soak my weary bones under a scalding shower, dress quickly, spend ten freezing minutes removing the constantly accumulating snow from the windshield and rear window of my car, and grope my way back home, fast, before the mounting snowdrifts make driving impossible. Even as I leave my car in the garage, I feel stiffness creeping into my joints, my back shows promise of tomorrow's torment. With a wry smile I inspect a swelling on my left elbow – a souvenir of a slip on the artificial turf, just before the last game. Now, the fire needs restocking. The Porto is still here, but what I need is a long drink. Water. I'm thirsty after the workout. I collapse in front of the dying fire. I'm too weary to stoke it.

A while back I had no problems.

Now, the aches are spreading their tentacles all-over my body. Yet, I am filled with a strange sense of achievement, a strange serenity that seems to more than compensate for my self-imposed efforts of the last few hours. Even the creeping stiffness seems welcome. For some unknown reason, it is good to be alive. Life *is* beautiful!

What are problems?

Why do people create them, needlessly, deliberately, without any apparent rhyme or reason? What lifts us from the comfort of our passive, lackadaisical existence to challenge the upper reaches of the Rockies, to cross turbulent oceans, to reach out for the moon? Are we in search of pain, of anguish? Are we a race of masochists, incapable of enjoying the benefits of an advanced civilization? Are we daredevils endowed with courage but lacking imagination to foresee the dangers inherent in our impetuous nature?

Or are we free spirits in search of a new experience, of a challenge, of the joys apparently inherent in conquest. Perhaps it is not the mountains, the oceans, the space, we crave to conquer. Perhaps we need to overcome the belief in our limitations. Perhaps we aspire to be as gods – free, unlimited, intrepid, undaunted.

But mostly free.

No matter how illogical our daring actions, how ill-advised the challenges we cast into the face of adversity, we all seem to manifest an inner need to taste the forbidden fruit. This need certainly does not originate in our minds, in our sense of logic. Our experience, instinct, pulls us towards the safe, the predictable. The more material our nature, the more staid, more stagnant we become. Some call it "old before our time". The established, the secure, hate change. The "money", the international markets, the capitalistic power-brokers, hate and fear unpredictability. A quarter-point fluctuation in the rates of interest can, and does, send the money markets into frenzy. For them, change is to be avoided. Stability is all. Strangely enough, this same premise has been the very essence of communism. They, *en masse*, would rather have protected what little they had than venture into the unknown. There is so little difference between people whose existence is dependent on material goods. They are all so very, very... predictable.

And money mongers are not alone. The leaders of any and all organizations, from the proud governments of great democracies, to the puffed-up generals of banana republics, to the elders of all the major churches – they all wallow in stability. They also lean heavily on tradition, on the past, on the proven and safe. Their minute, puny concessions to evolution is regarded, by their followers, as evidence of flexibility. But leopards cannot lose their spots. Likewise the bigwigs, chiefs, dignitaries, eminencies, nabobs, barons, czars, magnates, moguls... are as afraid of change, any change, as the devil is of holy water. They are all afraid to lose power. And it is power, not money, which is at the root of all evil. Power subjugates Spirit, and Spirit is the essence of freedom. The great, new horizons are invariably conquered by the most unorthodox individuals, never by the upholders of the *status quo*.

Our heart is where our treasure is. And the treasure of all organizations lies in the past – in the power-base developed over the years. This is true of any power-structure, including religions. The *raison d'être of* any organization is the long-term control of it's members. This, once again, is equally true of *all* international conglomerates, be they political, commercial or ecclesiastic. Yet the treasure of the human heart is in the realm of freedom. Freedom to face the unknown. The human spirit shall not be constrained, subdued, enslaved, subjugated by repression, by threats of exile or excommunication.

Spirit, like freedom, shall not be bridled.

Over the years, I observed that all that aspire to the spiritual realm, to a higher state of consciousness, dread the doldrums of stasis. They dread the *absence* of problems! They live for the challenge. They know that change is the very essence of growth, of improvement. They know that problems are granted freely only to those still in the kindergarten; whereas they, the awakened, have outgrown this privilege. They must now draw their own challenges from the Field of Inexhaustible Opportunities. They are now learning how to stretch their own potential to the very limits – and then – beyond.
Problem is a concomitant of change. Change is an expression of life itself. And life is the greatest challenge of all.

I observed these intoxicating souls, and then I discovered their secret.
After struggling half my life with ever mounting problems, I decided, once and for all, to eliminate them from my life. Every one of them. All it required was a change in attitude. I began treating them, those ostensible problems, as opportunities. It sounded good but – something was still missing. And then I had it! The missing wisp of wisdom gave me courage to put this premise into practice. I realized that facing a challenge is no more than facing a new, hitherto unknown, state of consciousness. This knowledge, as though by magic, converted problems into challenges, and those into opportunities. I also learned that I can enter such new states of consciousness for as long as I choose. Not a second longer.
I haven't had a problem since.

***
970324

44

SANCTIFYING

Sanctifying is synonymous with making holy, and holy means whole or complete. To sanctify anyone, anything, any trait is to make him, her, or it, complete. When such state or condition is achieved, then, and only then are we free to move onto other, more demanding challenges. And this is what life is all about.

Simple.

We are born with a powerful awareness of our origin. It is a remnant, a shadow, of the state of consciousness which we enjoyed before entering a "skin", a physical enclosure consisting of atoms held in a certain relationship to each other by information contained therein. The 'therein' is the knowledge inherent in the atoms and molecules, in the genetic code, and last but certainly not least, by our awareness. This last consists of two principle aspects. The conscious and the subconscious. The subconscious stores knowledge acquired over vast evolutionary periods. The conscious is that which we are here to work with. The conscious is the tip of the iceberg which, although but a tiny fraction of the total ice-mass (of information), is the only part which has its head above the water. It sees where it is going.

Or... it should.

As we become attracted by a new or perhaps a recurring trait crossing our stream of consciousness, we, by applying our experience, must work on it, so as to gain command over the particular attribute. When control is achieved, our work, on that particular trait, is complete. The trait has become sanctified. By this process, arduous, painstaking, but crowned with an enormous sense of achievement, we add an attribute to that aspect of our being which is immortal. The new, sanctified trait becomes integrated into that which we call soul. In the more down-to-earth terminology, the trait is also imprinted in or on our subconscious, and all our behaviour will henceforth be coloured by its presence.

The good news, as already mentioned, is that we shall never lose this trait. It becomes part of our kingdom, of our indestructible possession. The not-so-good news is that there are an infinite number of traits to work on, and.... there are also *degrees* of wholeness, or perfection. What is quite saintly to some may not be quite as perfect to others. But in a very peculiar way.

Think of Euclid. He created geometry that stood the test of time. Children, of all ages sill learn his methods, sill study and pass tests in knowledge of Euclidean geometry. Sounds pretty perfect. It is. At a certain level of understanding. For as good as Euclidean geometry is in solving problems of our everyday life, it is utterly useless when applied to cosmological problems, where Einsteinian geometry holds sway. We might say that at certain level of understanding the first concept has been sanctified, made whole for the purposes of the day in hand but, as we grow and mature in our interests, in our search for knowledge, we must once again start from scratch, learn new methods, acquire new skills and make them our own. Our grandchildren shall struggle with geometries we have never heard of. And so on. Forever.

The same applies to the more intangible traits. While no temporal organization, (including most marriages) would survive without the ability to compromise, this same trait is anathema to spiritual life. What is near perfect at the emotional or mental levels is very imperfect in the spiritual or cosmic realm. At higher levels of understanding compromise is

quite unacceptable.
We cannot serve two masters.[189]

Whenever we choose to abide in a down-to-earth state of consciousness, the old, Euclidean geometry is as good as ever. When we reach higher... well, it simply doesn't work. This cyclic rise in our understanding of the universe is exemplified in the cycles of the Zodiac, which, time after time, guide us over similar territories (states of consciousness) but put before us greater problems to solve, greater degrees of wholeness to be achieved. And, it bears repeating, there is no end to this journey. Perhaps this is why most of us regard the concept of God as the Infinite. Infinite as well as Eternal.

We already know that the only true way to *really* learn anything is to become one (to fully identify) with the object of our study. Rather than reading about golf, let's play the game. Rather than reading books on how to paint, let's smudge some oil on our canvas. Sure we can read about it. But a thousand books about the technique of playing the violin will not give us as much as a few lessons with a good teacher. The same is true of the more intangible traits. We can read a great deal about countless saints. But books will not sanctify us. Acting as though we were saints, will. Permanently. There is one technique that does help though. The mystics discovered it millennia ago. The technique is called contemplation. Think of flying. But don't contemplate how to fly. Just spread your wings and.... ...and become the object of your contemplation. Not an eagle – not even the wind. Become complete. Whole. In your heart, become flight itself. You can do it. Or at least, your soul can. And aren't you and your soul one?

---

[189] *"No man can serve two masters: for either he will hate the one, and love the other; or else he will hold to the one, and despise the other. Ye cannot serve God and mammon."* [Matthew 6: 24]. No compromise whatsoever is possible in spiritual matters. I met people of above average intelligence who were quite unable to understand this postulate.

All pilgrims who imagine that one day they will achieve perfection will be forever disappointed. There is no level, no state of consciousness that can be said to be the highest achievable. Those among us, who assign human traits to gods, succeed only in limiting their own, personal concept of their god. Sooner or later we all realize that we cannot define that which is beyond limitations. Spinoza saw that many centuries ago. The Christ, well before him, said that none is perfect but the Father, and He is in heaven.[190] The Father, in Christ's teaching referred to the Spirit. To that which IS. We, all of us, no matter how holy, how saintly, how spiritually elevated, we find our becoming within that Spirit. It is as though we were permanently immersed in an ocean of love and information. What changes is our understanding of the ocean, never the ocean Itself.

Anyone for a swim?

***

970327

The man to whom is unveiled the mystery of Love
Exists no longer, but vanishes into Love.
Place before the Sun a burning candle
And watch its brilliance disappear before that blaze.
The candle exists no longer,
it is transformed into Light;
There are no more signs of it,
it itself becomes sign.

Jalal-ud-Din Rumi[191]

---

[190] Compare Matthew 19:17
[191] Harvey, Andrew LIGHT UPON LIGHT, Inspirations from RUMI, [North Atlantic Books, California 1996] pg.79.

45

SILENCE

To get any service, any service at all, press button 1-to-a-100. Then hold the receiver close to your ear, so that we can pump you full of noise. Vulgar, senseless, obscene noise. The scourge of our age. Alexander Graham Bell is turning in his grave. So is Edison. So should be anyone invading our ears with impunity.

Silence is golden, the sages affirm sternly.

It doesn't make any money, counter the media producers?

To whom are we to listen? *A blooming peace shall ever bless thy morn*, Prior assures us.[192] Have Euterpe and Terpsichore forsaken us?[193] Noise, din and clamour. The unholy trinity. Noise makes a lot of money, the highest of man's aspirations. It seems that most of us have already lost the ability to listen our own thoughts, let alone to the deep silence at the centre of our being.

"Be still, and know that I am God."[194] Be still? How can we, with all the bedlam around us. *But I want to be heard,* cry thousands hungry for their share of the pie. Never mind if we've earned it. *We have a right!* A right at whose expense,

---

[192] Matthew Prior 1664-1721, English poet
[193] Euterpe is the muse of music or of lyric poetry, Terpsichore, her sister, of choral song and dance.
[194] Psalm 46:10

asked Ayn Rand?[195] A right to pollute our lives with noise? *Are we not all equal?* No, none of us are equal. Some of us talk and some listen. And all who talk have no opportunity to listen. They drown the silence with the sound of their own voices. *But we are so.... lonely. We want to share our thoughts, our feelings!*

Listen – and you'll be lonely no longer, answer the sages. Listen to the voice whispering within the silence of your heart. It too demands, begs, beseeches to be heard. But you're not listening. You are too busy talking. *And I said, and she said, and I said, and he said....* They all talked – none listened. *I'll see you! We'll TALK some more the next time! We'll do lunch. So much to tell you...*

But who will give *us* ear?

I no longer derive pleasure from the majority of TV programs. Imagine... the dreamy serenity of the Serengeti... the majesty of pristine icebergs rose-tinted by the setting sun... a set of sails weaving their whispering way across the endless ocean... industrious insects going about their buzzing business deep within the summer's eve. Peace, serenity interspaced with silence. Technology gave us such a marvelous opportunity to bring nature into our homes. And then a "music" director superimposes on these priceless wonders his own noise, evocative of lugubrious wailing, invariably accompanied by a frying pan smashing against a brick wall in primitive, barbaric rhythm. Please, don't misunderstand me, Mr. Director. I love music. Wolfgang Amadeus is a dear friend of mine. You, Mr. Music Director, are no Mozart.

And why? Does not nature provide us with her own symphonic poems?

---

[195] ATLAS SHRUGGED by Ayn Rand, [Random House, New York 1957]

Aspiring figure skaters spent hundreds, perhaps thousands arduous, painstaking hours harmonizing their intricate movements with the music. And then a stone deaf, egotistical TV bigmouth overrides the artists' work with the sound of his or her pernicious, arrogant, insidious yapping. Why? Don't they know we also have screens at home, which we can see for ourselves? That we are neither blind, deaf nor stupid?

And all this Hollywood tinsel... Why must it all be glutted with cantankerous noise? Shootings, explosions, the screech of tires, car smashes, screams, wailing and general bedlam. The flashing coruscations as offensive to our eyes as the sound-track to our ears. And all this peppered by most horrible noise of "beat" thrashing the devil's rhythm on our long-suffering eardrums. Why? Why do they hate us so?

Has the world gone mad?

Stilling, or at least reducing, our contribution to the generation of noise is but a first step towards opening the floodgates of one's inner silence. Anyone who succeeded, even momentarily, to still the current of his or her thoughts, soon discovered that silence is so much more than just an absence of noise. How are we to listen to our own Selves with all this confusion within us?

The highest form of prayer is silence.

Not just verbal, mechanical or "instrumental" silence, but the much deeper, more internalized silence. A silence which stills the clutter of the mind. The Bible is replete with references to this unwelcome clamour. Jeremiah calls it the *tumultuous ones*, meaning incessant thoughts.[196] Isaiah compares it to a *tumultuous city* – 'city' symbolizing a state of consciousness; elsewhere he likens it to the *roaring of the sea*,[197] with the 'sea' symbolizing the mental aspect of human nature. When King David pleads with us to *be still and know*

---

[196] Jeremiah 48:45
[197] Isaiah 5:30

... he refers to the stillness within, to an inner silence which is the prerequisite to the eventual discovery of who we really are. All to whom the sound of their own voice overrides the desire to hear the silence within shall never achieve this knowledge. At least, not in their present lifetime. And certainly not in the glittery escapism of the Hollywood induced illusion.

The sages are right. The Silence is golden. It is of purest gold.

***
970331

*"But the Lord is in his holy temple:
let all the earth keep silence before him."*

Habakkuk
2:20

46

PARALLEL EVOLUTION

Heaven and earth. Spirit and matter. Possibility and fulfilment. The first dyad refers to the antipodal states of consciousness. The second to that in which the state of consciousness finds it's being. The third to the creative process which is the substance of evolution.

The dance of evolution. The going out and the coming in.

Parallel Evolution begins when the conscious takes over from the subconscious. In human terms, it occurs when man, a soul embodied in human flesh, gains first awareness of its origin.[198] Until this moment, the evolutionary movement was centrifugal, away from the centre of origin. It started with the Big Bang and it followed the dictates of the expanding universe. This flow, referred to in the Bible as the Law, controls all nature, all aspects of the manifested universe. In metaphysical terms, man's pre-self-realization stage, together with the rest of the animal kingdom, is controlled exclusively by, for the want of a better word, the "subconscious" of God. This phase of evolution can be said to be set on automatic. Nothing can change its course. The inexorability of this law

---

[198] The word "man" is used generically. It represents an androgynous being which, in any particular reincarnation, can manifest predominance of either male or female characteristics.

is confirmed in the Bible, among others, in the following passages: It is easier for heaven and earth to pass, than one tittle of the law to fail.[199] Or: I came to fulfil the law, not to destroy it.[200] It is this act of fulfilment of the Law that exonerates the change in the direction of the evolution of man's consciousness, ultimately of human race. The switch-over from the automatic or subconscious to the wilful or conscious mode of being.

Man, his new realization contesting the inexorable forces of physical evolution applies the breaks and slowly turns the rudder to point in the opposite direction. Until this point in his evolution, man is subject to all the laws that, contrary to the egotistical promulgation of some sacerdotal casts, deny him any expression of free will, any untrammelled self-expression. Until this point man is subject to the stringent laws of kill or be killed, of survival of the fittest, which continues to govern the consciousness of the vast majority of the human and all other species to this day. For the most part, man still remains a puppet controlled by the strings of the evolutionary forces. The purpose of this, the material evolution, is to provide, develop and sustain a vehicle which will enable soul (awareness) to initiate, develop and sustain Parallel Evolution. This new direction is not regressive, but is characterized by a condition wherein the spiritual content forming the embodied consciousness shall be on the increase. The "vehicle" continues on its way. This new direction is thus completely independent of the evolutionary forces, nor does it in any way counteract its laws. It is the Spiritual versus the Material evolution. The centripetal or integrating, as against the centrifugal or dispersing. The Spiritual leading to Oneness, the Material to variety and fragmentation. Soul is One, but it finds expression in infinite diversity.

---

[199] Luke 16:17
[200] compare Matthew 5:17

The theory of the oscillating universe is well known. We, human micro-universes, perform an oscillating dance of binary states of consciousness.

To this end man is provided with boundless possibilities. Boundless oceans of information. Countless states of consciousness already created, ready for man to enter, to become one with, at his leisure. In this alone man retains his free will. He cannot deny his destiny, but he can choose his time. *There is no time in eternity*. But he needn't worry about having a suitable vehicle – its future is assured. Darwin asserts: "Hence we may look with some confidence to a secure future of great length. And as natural selection works solely by and for the good of each being, all corporeal and mental endowments will tend to progress towards perfection."[201] Darwin chooses not to mention that mental endowments are an integral part of the material universe.

At the point when the change in the evolutionary direction takes place, man becomes aware of the Ocean of Endless Possibilities. He becomes aware and is awed by the sudden awareness of order, harmony, balance, Divine Laws resulting unavoidably in prolific Beauty. This nascent realization grows, matures, gradually sublimates all previous views of the universe. Until this moment, the embodied consciousness was not capable of recognizing the wonder of creation. It may be unwise to assume that the return trip, the Parallel Evolution, would be much shorter than that which brought us from Eden to this point in our awareness.

Knowledge is that which keeps evolution on an even keel. Love is that which binds it together; it is the gathering the centripetal Force. It draws, with ever increasing intensity, until all is gathered, all is brought back to its point of origin. Like a universal Black Hole. Nothing escapes from its over-

---

[201] Darwin, Charles ORIGIN OF SPECIES (publ. in 1859)

powering attraction. As men, we cannot know what happens at its enigmatic centre. What happens in the Heart of God? Not even Light escapes It, not even ultimate divine Knowledge. The best we can hope for is to meet and observe the rare souls that approach the end of their return journeys. We must always remain aware that their was not a journey in time, nor in space, but a journey within an ocean of consciousness. We can bask in the reflected light of their knowledge, be drawn by the love emanating from their core. They are the Beacons, the Way-showers, the Paragons of Evolution.

The Parallel Evolution. The evolution in Spirit.

Where they lead, we must follow. It is the nature of our being.

And what then? What of the Light at the Heart of a Black Hole?

At some fleeting instant of yet another eternity, when all is gathered, bathed in the bliss of Oneness, saturated with such Love as to be no longer containable within the affluence of Singularity of Being.... That which is ONE shall explode. And time will start again, expand into new space, and foster new evolution. Billions of years later Adam shall reach the stage when his subconscious, his animal soul, shall add substance to his being. And then a new, a fragile infant shall be born in his heart, a new awareness, that of a child longing to return home.

And he will spin the web of an ascending spiral, the eternal dance of Love, in search of the essence of Being.

***

970407

Kiciuni, na rocznicę

47

ADAM

And God created Adam.
God also created the evolutionary process. Few would argue against the thesis that all within the universe originates from a Single Source. The religionists call this source God, the scientists the Cosmic Egg.[202] Religionists endow their God with divergent, often infinite attributes, and then force others to accept the image they created. The scientists study the divergence and learn by observing the diversity of (God's) Creation. Their search for the Truth includes repeated attempts to synthesize all into One.[203] We can speculate if Adam was the result of a Conscious act of God or, of what might be referred to as, an act of the Divine Subconscious, i. e. of an evolutionary process.

Human pride calls for Divine intervention in Adam's arrival on this earth. In fact, most of the religionists insist on it. They like to call themselves Creationists. The pride inherent in such a posture might well be enough for the scientists to reject their thesis. They much prefer the evolutionary stance.

There is a third alternative.

We could also assume that the reality in which we exist is the result of an accident. That the endless universes, galaxies, stars and solar systems – all held in accidental gravita-

---

[202] The progenitor of the Big Bang
[203] The long awaited Unified Field Theory.

tional and electromagnetic fields – are all subjects to accidentally indomitable laws. That the prolific realms of flora and fauna guided on their path by accidental forces resulted in an accidental evolution of Adam. We can assume all that. We can also assume that we need our heads examined. Although, under the circumstances, why bother.

We might as well stop the accidentally spinning world and get off!

Does it all matter? Is the Divine any less Divine in whatever form It chooses to manifest Itself? Aren't the scientists, the astrophysicists, anthropologists, palaeontologists, and what-have-you-ists more competent to speculate on Adam's arrival on earth then the religionists? Don't their intricate titles command as much respect as those usurped by the heads of various faiths? Assuming that most of us reject the prospect of being bastards (the third alternative), must we choose among the remaining two?

No. Not if we delve deeper into the first couple of chapters of Genesis. The religionists and the scientists are both wrong. And I'll be shot for daring to suggest it!

The Creationists, basing their "knowledge" on faith, like to ignore the evidence of their senses. They imitate ostriches, until the pressure of common sense forces them to release a little of their ill-begotten ignorance. Vatican's recent concession on treating the theory of evolution as an "acceptable alternative" (to what?) speaks for itself. And for as long as the leaders of religions continue to insist that the Bible is a scientific exposé, they will continue to wallow in their ignorance.

The Bible is a book dealing with the Spiritual, not the material. With the Cause, not with the effect. It deals with states of consciousness, not with mental, emotional or physical phenomena. When it touches on the mundane, it is only for the purposes of an illustration. At this very rudimentary level the Bible tackles the issue of Adam.

The Bible takes up the story of Adam at the point when God created him in his image. God had NOT created a living, walking Adam. He created a single state of consciousness that was both male *and* female.[204] An androgynous STATE OF CONSCIOUSNESS. Only later this entity had been enclosed in a material form. God gathered "dust of the ground, and breathed into his nostrils the breath of life". And only then "man became a living soul".[205]

Up to this instant of eternity, the universe, the stars and the earth, and things in it, existed only as states of consciousness. Only Adam's awareness gave earth physical reality. In fact, it was the product of his awareness. Adam became the cause (soul), and the result (physical manifestation). This serves to explain that the universe we perceive with our senses is only as real as we choose to make it. The universe of our dreams is as real as that of our waken state. The physical reality is that which we create. Each one for each individual self. We each are Adam, an androgynous entity. An embodiment of soul, capable of entering an infinite number of states of consciousness.

Einstein gave us the famous $E=MC^2$ formula. It seems incomprehensible to most. Yet all it really means is that matter and energy are interchangeable. That that which we perceive as matter can be expressed, mathematically, as energy. As an intangible, ineffable field held in place by an act of our consciousness. Not mind but consciousness. It is this breath of life, this ability to recognize true reality that makes us different from the rest of the creatures of earth. If we cannot recognize it, then we are NOT different from the beast. We do, however, retain a latent potential to do so. When we do, we become Adam. God is not a Concept that exists and acts in the past. It is a Concept beyond time. It is a Principle as

---

[204] Genesis 1:27
[205] ibid 2:7

active today as in Biblical times. The process of creation is over (states of consciousness), the present evolutionary process has just began.

Once Adam became self-aware, he developed a subconscious (Eve), which became the storage-house of information necessary to sustain his embodiment. Knowledge was necessary to maintain his instrument of learning (physical body). This knowledge would be useless if he could not differentiate between good and evil. What is good and what is evil in the material sense. Hence the tree of knowledge. It is amusing that most religions equate the serpent with the devil. In Gnostic literature it is a symbol for divine wisdom!

Until Adam ate off the tree of knowledge he was an innocent. He could not recognize the nature of duality in the material universe. It is only when he accumulated knowledge in his subconscious that discernment or judgement became possible. All judgement is a matter of comparison between the opposites. And opposites can exist only in a dualistic state of consciousness. Of course, the loss of innocence was an unavoidable concomitant of this condition.

The Torah also asserts that if Adam eats of the tree of knowledge he will surely die[206]. In the Bible, dying invariably refers to *spiritual* death, i.e. a loss of awareness of the Spiritual reality. It happens when we recognize the material world as real. The true reality is ONE, beyond the concepts of duality. It is fascinating to note that it is Adam's subconscious (Eve) which recognizes this necessity for the maintenance of the vehicle for his growth. Remember Adam is a state of consciousness endowed with self-awareness. A soul – temporarily embodied.

To sum up, the Biblical story of Adam is a detailed de-

---

[206] ibid 2:17 In Hebrew, he words are: dying you shall die, suggesting that as we sink deeper into materiality we progressively loose contact with (spiritual) reality.

scription of our rudimentary evolution. First we are an idea (an androgynous being, spirit). Then, a physical body is constructed (earth, gestation period). Then, "the body" becomes aware of being alive (the breath of life enters the physical body), and finally we develop the subconscious (Eve, animal soul). What a pity that all this leads to a slow death, a slow descent into the abyss of materiality. Yet, it seems the only way to learn. Or at least, the quickest.

But then, one day, we shall find a saving grace, the Tree of Life. The tree which floods us with Light.

But that's another story.

***

970408

The problem is that the paths which this light should take are blocked with falsehood and darkness.
After all, light and darkness cannot coexist any more than God and creatures can.
If God is to enter, then the creatures must leave.

Meister Eckhart
[Eckhart Von Hochheim]
c.1260 – 1327

*I have met people who are beautiful, intelligent,
rich, and gracious, who seem to have everything,
but who lack the mysterious sincerity
essential for the Path.
And I have met people who seemed to be wrecks
and have nothing – neither elegance nor beauty
nor attractive intelligence – and yet the Pearl sat
in the palm of their hands,
because Love was in their hearts,
and in its full passion.*

Jalal-ud-Din Rumi
[THE PEARL]

The only real valuable thing is intuition

Albert Einstein

---

[207] Harvey, Andrew LIGHT UPON LIGHT, Inspirations from RUMI, [North Atlantic Books, California 1996] pg.75.

48

GRACE

By the grace of the King. The Queen. By His, Her or Your Highness. There is a day of grace, when sinners may obtain forgiveness. There are three days of grace of legal absolution. One can be in the bad, good and presumably indifferent graces of almost anyone. And one can suffer any and all of the above with bad grace, or good grace. There is an awful lot of grace around...

There is also Divine Grace.

A very different kind of Grace. It cannot be granted nor taken away. It cannot be pursued, bought, or acquired by holy or unholy means. It is neither awarded nor bestowed for services rendered.

Divine Grace IS.

Like all Divine attributes, Grace just is. Even as Spirit is. Love is. Life is. It cannot be fragmented, divided, increased nor decreased. All the Divine attributes just ARE. That is what makes them Divine. That is also what makes them integral, indivisible, indestructible, omnipresent, eternal. They just ARE. Just as God, the Divine, the Eternal, the Principle, the Ocean of Love and Mercy, by whatever Name – IT just IS.

I AM THAT I AM.

Nothing has changed. The Divine never changes. What changes is the degree of our realization of It. Of That which is within us. And without us. Our consciousness changes or more correctly, we change our awareness of different states of being – at will. States of consciousness are like rooms in the house of God, or houses standing in a divine garden. A truly great state of consciousness has been described as a great city, Jerusalem. The City of Peace. Divine Peace. Nothing to do with the Jews or the Palestinians. This ability to enter different states of being, of awareness, is an attribute of the divine within us. No political system, no religious regime, no prison cell, can withdraw from us that which is divine.

Likewise, Grace is a divine State of Consciousness.

If a man refuses to switch on the light in a house fully wired for electricity, fitted with all the necessary outlets, abundant in magnificent fixtures all plugged in and ready to shine, he cannot complain for staying in the dark. Grace is like that. All we have to do is to switch It on. It is available to absolutely everybody at absolutely all times. We are all fitted with all the attributes necessary to enjoy the abundance of It. All we must do is to enter Its realm. And... accept It.

Our house is our personal state of consciousness. It is that in which we spend our life. It is that which gives us awareness of our existence. We can keep it dark, with the blinds tightly drawn. We can let the light in and rejoice in its abundance. It is our house and we are its masters. Or should be. There is no difference between a castle and a humble shack. What changes is our perception. A shack is a palace to some, a hovel to another. A kingdom can dwarf us with its attendant responsibilities. A humble cottage can afford us freedom. The choice is ours. We can choose to live within transient illusions of poverty or glory, and suffer the darkness of our ignorance.

We can also elect to live in a State of Grace.

GRACE

Grace is omnipresent.

It is not reserved for the few, nor is it restricted to religious orders, nor is it kept on a leash of sacerdotal merchants. A drunk in a gutter may face the steel bars of a forbidding grating or turn his eyes towards the infinity of the sky above him. There is no more Grace in a church resplendent with the vanity of gilt statues than in a New York slum or Brazilian favelas. The pauper can have his heart lined with purest gold, a billionaire may be held in shackles of distrust, worry, greed and loneliness. The abundance of Grace has no limits. No barriers. It courts no favourites. It is open to all.

But we must turn the switch.

So what is this attribute sought by so many, enjoyed by so few? What is this magic awareness of saints, envied by the masses? As mentioned before, Grace cannot be pursued. It cannot be achieved by prayer, exercise, sacrifice, starvation nor any form of self-denial. All these are physical functions and mental contrivances. Grace is beyond our sensibilities, beyond the intrinsic duality of human perception. It is beyond logic. It is that state of consciousness that opens our inner vision to the Truth. It makes it possible for us to experience the world, people, nature, abundance within and without us, as it really is; to consciously become an integral element of the incredible diversity in which the Divine manifests Its Presence. When we enter this elusive state, we cannot distinguish ourselves from the Whole. We are complete, as the world is complete. We step, lightly, beyond the limitations of time and space. This is the state of Grace. We dwell in It for sequential fractions of eternity. And we share it with others – as all are also there – unbeknownst to their minds and bodies. Yet they are all there. As Soul.

Relationships intricate beyond reason, sublime harmony, immutable balance – all resulting in an overpowering awareness of beauty – all form part of this, the True Reality. It is ever within our grasp; It dwells within the stillness of our heart. All we must do is to raise the veil protecting It from the profane. The veil of our ego. It is ours to behold. It is where our true Self resides. All we must do is to become one with It.

I never said it was easy.

***

970410

*"Whoever possesses God in their being, has him
in a divine manner,
and he shines out to them in all things;
for them all things taste of God
and in all things it is God's image that they see"*

Meister Eckhart
[Eckhart Von Hochheim]
c.1260 – 1327

49

SALVATION

When I hold down the "power key" and then press the letter "s", I protect my work from annihilation. From death. My computer does the actual saving but I know exactly what I have saved, and why I considered it worthwhile to do so. I seldom save work in progress. I wait until the computer screen reflects the very best I can do and then, and only then, I perform my act of salvation. My poem, my article, an essay, whatever the endeavour, will never be erased, never cease to exist. It became a permanent electronic imprint in the memory storage. I can shut off the computer but the work will live on. It became immortal. At least, by computer standards.

By contrast, when the captain of a forlorn boat blown off-course on the seven seas radios S O S., the distress signal meaning Save Our Souls, he has little concern for his soul. What he wants saved is his body. His flesh and blood. Yet, though expressed perhaps over-dramatically, he does know what he wants saved.

On the other hand when the priesthood of various religions advocate their followers to save their soul, confusion sets in. What do they mean, exactly? Didn't they tell us that our souls are immortal? Surely, if something is impregnable and indestructible, it needs no saving. It is eternally protected by its very nature. "Ah!" they say craftily, "Your soul may be immortal but it can suffer an eternal death!" Now this sounds like a mumbo-jumbo to rival the best of the political speeches. Eternal death? Immortal? Make up your mind, gentlemen. What is it that you want saved? And what for? Are you sure it is worth saving? What if I save my soul only to spend eternity eating fire and brimstone, wouldn't I rather let my soul die than let it suffer forever? Please, let's be serious.

The blind leading the blind....

Yet none need suffer from this myopic confusion. The Bible, on which many of the churches claim to base their authority, is quite clear on the subject, and quite at odds with the teaching of every Christian sect that I ever came in contact with. To clear up this matter we must establish, as clearly as we can, what we mean by a soul, what is it that we want saved, how to go about it, and why.

The soul, as defined in the Bible, is NOT immortal. The Bible refers to our soul as *nephesh*, a Hebrew word meaning *animal* soul.[208] And animal soul is the repository of all that we, as individuals, as units of consciousness, have accumulated since our emergence from the primordial slime which mother earth stirred and gurgled in her sulphurous bowels. As micro-organisms, as more complex biological structures, as fish and fowl, as animals, primates and humans. It could be said that our soul is our private world, our individual universe. Long before we gained conscious awareness of the Divine Spark enlivening our bodies, the Omnipresent Intelligence regarded us with benevolence, with infinite patience,

---

[208] The Hebrew *nephesh* corresponds to the Greek *psuché*, or psyche, not to be confused with the Hebrew *neshamah* meaning breath, or the Greek *pneuma*, meaning breath of life or spirit.

with compassion and understanding. After all, isn't this how we now regard the animal kingdom? Don't we look upon the phenomena of nature as the repositories of individual states of consciousness, as our younger brothers and sisters? As tiny, growing, maturing souls... Animal souls?

Nephesh, our animal soul, is our subconscious.[209] It is the sum-total of all that makes us different from each other. It is the quintessence, the very substance, of our individuality. The Divine Spark within us is identical in every respect to every other Divine Spark in every other entity; in trees and flowers, in the sand along the endless ocean. In every single atom. Spirit is Spirit. It is permanent, static, indestructible. Spirit is Life Itself. Soul defines what we have accomplished under It's guidance. When Spirit vacates our bodies, we, as individuals, cease to exist. Unless.... Unless we save our souls.

Unless we save our souls.

Now we are getting an idea as to what is it that we are endeavouring to save. At any particular moment of our lives, we personify the sum-total *all that we ever were*. We are the best that we can possibly be, at this instant of our evolution. The positive traits we have accumulated form part of our permanent individuality. The rest, we pick-up from the ethers with each reincarnation, to work on again and again. Our failures are NOT part of our soul. But the *effects* of our failures vibrate in the inner space, and as we re-enter this world in seemingly endless cycles of reincarnations we are bound to repair the damage we have done to the fabric of the universe. We must convert our failures into triumphs. Then, and only then, our soul will incorporate them, as it's permanent treasure. It is a process of trial and error. We grow, we learn, we improve. We learn to save that which is of value, discard that which is not. Without a natural selection there would be no evolution. Could the Divine be any less demanding of our souls than of Mother Nature?

We are born, we learn, we die, we are born again.... we die again....

As we vacate our bodies, the Divine Sparks keeps that which is worth saving. That which is saved becomes our first step towards immortality. The rest is kept in a state of suspension, in waiting, and in our next life becomes part of us again. The subconscious lives on, even as our physical bodies disintegrate. It forms part of our inner body, which though not immortal, has a much longer shelf-life then our biological constructs. But they are NOT immortal. Immortality must be earned.

So how do we go about saving our soul? The *whole* soul? Where is the power button on the Divine Computer, to preserve our total being, our whole individuality? Can this really be done? Can we survive this life as "us"? As individuals? Can we die, approach our loved ones and say: "Be not afraid, it is I"?

We can.

We can gain Life by giving up life. We can decide that we prefer to be immortal rather than mortal. That *that* which is indestructible, eternal, that which is good is always better than that which is good only on occasion. On a Sunday. We can decide that that which is good for the Whole takes precedence over that which is good only for a part. We can choose to become permanent, uncompromising, inflexible ambassadors of Infinite Intelligence, of Divine Love. No matter what. And what happens then?

A very strange thing happens.

We, mortal souls, become indispensable. As we become pure channels for the Spirit, It refuses to give us up. It relishes the wondrous things It can accomplish with the attributes of Its host. It embraces the soul, our soul; It increases its vibrations until it becomes a Living Entity. There is a period of cleansing, of shedding the remnants of ego. The soul's vibrations now approach the velocity of light. It rises beyond the wiles, beyond the illusion of material existence. All the attributes of its individuality are fine-tuned. Chiselled, honed to perfection. They *all* become worth preserving. And then, the soul goes Nova. A blast of Divine Glory. It becomes one with the Presence which was its guide for countless millions of years.

They become One. Forever.

***

970418

A free man thinks of nothing less than of death;
and his wisdom is meditation not of death,
but of life.

Baruch Spinoza
(1632–1677)

*In our ecclesiastical region there are priests
who don't baptize the children of single mothers
because they weren't conceived in the sanctity of marriage.*

These are today's hypocrites.

*Those who clericalize the church. Those who separate
the people of God from salvation.*

Pope Francis

50

EVE

The first lady.
Far from being Adam's temptress, from being God's afterthought on a belated realization that Adam might be lonely, Eve carries a greater diversity of symbolic meaning than seems possible, until we take into account that the principle concern of biblical teaching is survival. And our survival depends wholly on our ability to raise our consciousness to a higher level. In this respect Eve is the fulcrum, the very axis on which the psychological universe turns.

Bible is a book replete with symbols. Deciphering them goes a long way towards assuring our continued existence.

When the Bible talks of Adam, it talks of "man" as a generic term for humanity. Let us remember that Adam was created a hermaphrodite: "male and female created he him".[210] In fact, initially, until "formed out of the ground", Adam was no more than a disembodied state of consciousness. Later he was furnished (evolved) with an animal soul, of which Eve became a symbol. From the anthropological point of view, Adam is every one of us – male and female. Eve, on the other hand, is always a woman. And, a great deal

---

[210] The Bible uses the pronoun "them" (Genesis 1:27), long before God created Eve (Genesis 2:21-22). I suggest that an early scribe compensated for his lack of understanding.

more.

A wise old lady told me recently that woman has been "called" to motherhood. I am sure that many women are. The elderly lady was presumably referring to a woman's body, hardly to her soul. To reduce the woman's stature to the functions of her womb is to negate the dignity of the Divine Spark within her. Woman is not just a fe-male prescribed by male sacerdotal lawmakers to be either a symbol of virginal purity or a machine to be used, again and again, by men, for the propagation of the species. Her body is endowed with the capability of bearing children, but it certainly is not limited to this function. Or to put it in yet another way, childbirth is the function of the vessel, not of the wine it contains. And it is the wine that bears witness to the secret knowledge.

Let us examine the biblical model of a woman a little more closely.

God, breathed (animal) soul into Adam's nostrils.[211]

But in the act of the creation of Eve, the Bible accomplishes three things: 1– it confirms the dualistic nature of man; 2– it furnishes us with a symbol for soul, in a way it's personification; and 3– with the creation of Eve, the Bible introduces the concept of the subconscious.

It is this subconscious that enables man to retain, store, and recall past experiences which will benefit and hopefully assure his survival. The subconscious is to man what memory storage is to a computer. If you accidentally erase the hard-disc with all the accumulated data, your computer's as good as useless. The hard-disc contains also all the software, the programs which render the computer useful. Without it... all is lost. It's as though we have lost our soul. No wonder Jesus said: "For what it profit a man if he shall gain the whole

---

[211] Genesis 2:7 The word *soul* is a translation of the Hebrew *nephesh*, meaning animal soul. It is important to distinguish this concept from the *El*, symbolizing the Divine Presence.

world and lose his own soul."[212] He would have no term of reference. No guidelines. He would be like a babe in arms. He would have to start again – from scratch. Generations of experience, of learning, of effort would be lost. Erased. Man would lose his ability to rely on his instinct. He wouldn't have any. We must look after our Eve. She is what makes us what we are. She is our individuality.

This is why the Bible attaches such great importance to the soul. At early stages of evolution, soul of man is hardly immortal. It is a mental construct, a field of information gathered and preserved by the sustaining, protective, and thus passive aspect of our nature. You might regard these to be feminine traits, and indeed, in the Bible a woman symbolizes these attributes. She is born of the consciousness of man and is inseparable part of him. That is why shall a "man leave his father and his mother (his attachments) and shall cleave unto his wife: and they shall be one flesh."[213] Only with Eve at his side, or more correctly, within his very flesh, is he complete.

This is the story of Eve. She and Adam are one. Like a man and his shadow.

Like a man and his soul.

We seldom wonder to what extend we rely on our subconscious. We seem to take our accumulated experience for granted. We forget that "Changes of circumstances and environment is the only constant in evolution".[214] In other words, the only certainty is the uncertainty. It's a vicious world out there. Dog eats dog. Darwin may have promulgated the survival of the fittest, but the Bible claims that the most experienced survive the best. Without Eve, we cannot survive.

But there is so much more to the soul.
The biblical Eve is a woman, wife, mother, a symbol of

---

[212] Mark 8:36
[213] Genesis 2:24
[214] *Creating the Creators* by Stephen Jay Gould, DISCOVER Oct. '96

the passive, but also the nurturing, the protecting aspect of the phenomenon of man. While the conscious mind tends to conquer new horizons, the subconscious, the woman, provides the home to come back to. She is the protected harbour in the stormy waters, the haven after a hard day's work, the castle offering peace and security.

Bible is a book dealing with the Spiritual, not the material. With the cause, not with the effect. It deals with states of consciousness. When it touches on the mundane, it is only to illustrate the results of not following its dictates. But it is concerned with man's welfare on earth. HERE and NOW. We are here to survive in the best, the most enjoyable way possible. The advocate of this premise said quite clearly, "These things have I spoken unto you, that your joy might remain in you, and that your joy might be full."[215]

It may come as a shock to many, particularly to the Christians, that survival, physical and spiritual, are not that far apart. The information contained in the genetic code (the DNA) is nature's way of storing the data necessary for survival. We forget that the molecules, the atoms, the subatomic particles, even the various fields of energy, all contain information on survival. The information is built into their very nature. One might say, that the information therein is the Subconscious of God. The Infinite Field of Information. Divine Intelligence. We, as individuals, reflect this Principle by storing our own data in, what the Bible calls, the animal soul. We store it, we constantly upgrade it, and we make daily selections, alterations and permutations of various interrelationships. We are each a tiny universe, independent yet extant in a field relative to all the other universes.

Next to our own survival, we have but one function in this life; and that is, to raise our subconscious to such a level as to make it indispensable to the universe. Eve, the symbol for our soul, is unique. There is a plethora of redundancy in

---

[215] John 15:11

the world: a safety margin built-in on a divine scale. But our souls are unique. Each one is created for a purpose, and without it's contribution, the universe would be incomplete. The United Negro College have a motto: "Mind is a terrible thing to waste". It is. Soul is part of our mind. One day, we shall all rely on intuitive knowledge. We shall learn to trust the silent voice at the core of our being. But to survive until then, we need lots and lots of experience. We need soul. We need our wife. We need Eve.

***
970420

...there are four stages in (anima's) development.
The first stage is best symbolized by the figure of Eve,
which represents purely instinctual and biological relations.
The second (Faust's Helen)... personifies a romantic and aesthetic level...
The third... the Virgin Mary – a figure who raised love (Eros) to the height of spiritual devotion.
The fourth ... is symbolized by Sapientia, wisdom transcending even the most holy and the most pure.

M.-L. von Franz
The Process of Individuation
216

---

[216] Jung, Carl, G. MAN AND HIS SYMBOLS [Dell publ. Co. New York 1979] pg.195

51

THE UNIVERSAL
AND
THE PARTICULAR

I and my Father are one.
Sometimes, in the affairs of man, a wondrous event occurs. The universal and the particular merge. The most miraculous event to manifest itself in the consciousness of mankind. It never lasts. It comes and goes like a comet. Prodigious, spectacular, surprising, wonderful, awing, phenomenal, shedding light, intangible yet real. To our forefathers – supernatural. Yet the event is so short, so ephemeral, that in spite of its glory many people fail to notice it. And those who do notice do so only after the fact.

Pity.

Perhaps the event is beyond the understanding of even the greatest minds. The Whole expresses Itself through one of Its parts. The two become one – qualitatively the same, quantitatively the part remaining insignificant. The message having been delivered, the messenger fades into oblivion. What remains is our hunger, our inexplicable longing for his divine attributes, his superhuman powers, knowing naught about his real personality. "Tribal or local heroes, such as the emperor Huang Ti, Moses, or the Aztec Tezcatlipoca, commit their boons to a single folk; universal heroes – Mohammed, Jesus,

Gautama Buddha – bring a message for the entire world".[217] None of the heroes are greater than their Master.[218] A part cannot be greater than the Whole. Yet for that fleeting instant, the two merged. A particular experienced the Universal. The rest of us seem destined to sate our hunger through the diversity of Its expression. The diversity of creation. If one could experience the totality of he universe, simultaneously, one would see the Face of God. It stands to reason that this cannot be accomplished with physical senses. What then? Are we destined to tread water forever?

That which is universal we call Whole, or Holy. And that which is "holiest" we call God. With our minds we can experience parts of the universe, whereas the realization of God reaches beyond the mind. Krishnamurti said: "To go beyond the mind there must be a cessation of the self, the "me". It is only then that That which we all worship, seek, comes into being."[219] And when that happens, the Universal merges with the particular.

The Father and I become one.

The prophets assert that to reach this state of consciousness we must keep still. We must not think but *know*. We must still our *minds* and reach a condition of absolute silence. When King David admonishes us to "be still and know that I am God,"[220] he talks about the stillness of the mind. The Bible, least of all the Psalms, is not concerned with physical agitation. The scriptures of all religions start with the mind and work "upwards". Krishnamurti, mentioned above, said

---

[217] Campbell, Joseph THE HERO WITH A THOUSAND FACES [Princeton University Press, © 1949 by Bollingen Foundation Inc., New York, N.Y]. (pg.38)

[218] John 5:19

[219] Jayakar, Pupul KRISHNAMURTI, a biography [Harper & Row, San Francisco, © 1986 by Pupul Jayakar]

[220] Psalm 46:10

that this condition of stillness, or as he calls it silence, is a precarious mode: that "any form of resistance destroys this state".

Yet, it is possible. It is the heritage of mankind.

The reason why man apparently finds it so difficult to understand this concept is because we create gods in our own image. We take our human attributes, increase them manifold and call the creation of our minds: god. An anthropomorphic god. We find his variegated images in countless churches and temples the world over, where thousands make millions by exploiting the masses. Yet in order to achieve the state of unity with the Infinite, the Whole, the first thing we must do is to shed all material attributes. We must cease to be that which we are, which we have become, and reverse the direction of our perceptions. Instead of looking out, we must look in. That which we search is not plastered on canonical walls; it is omnipresent. Thus – IT is also within us.

The merging of consciousness within the biblical "bridal chamber"[221] must be tempered by the understanding of the relation between the knower and the known. The founder of the International Society for Krishna Consciousness puts it as follows: "In the relative world the knower is different from the known, but in the Absolute Truth both the knower and the known are one and the same thing." I suspect that most of us are firmly anchored in the relative world! The Swami continues: "In the relative world the knower is the living spirit or superior energy, whereas the known is inert matter or inferior energy."[222] Before we can enter the bridal chamber, the du-

---

[221] We have strayed a long way from the original, biblical meaning of the bridegroom and the bride. The Hebrew *chathan* translated as "bridegroom", means one who contracts affinity. The Hebrew *kallah*, translated as "bride", in fact means the complete or perfect one.

[222] SRIMAD BHAGAVATAM, compiled by His Divine Grace A.C. Bhaktivendanta Swami Prabhupada. [© 1978 Bhaktivedanta Book Trust.] (pg. 104)

ality of the material world must be erased from our consciousness. Once we recognize ourselves for what we really are, we begin our return journey – back to our source.

It is amazing how many of us insist on identifying with the inert matter, with the swirling atoms that combine to form our bodies. We insist that we are what we eat. Einstein's assurances regarding the interchangeability of matter and energy does not seem to spur us on.[223] At best, we identify with our minds (I think, therefore I am[224]), without realizing that the mind relies heavily on the subconscious, which in turn is preoccupied with the preservation and maintenance of the biological constructs we occupy.

Yet we do not have to be imprisoned, life after life, in this cycle of ignorance.

All it takes is a *conscious* decision. We must decide, as an act of our will, that we shall identify with the spiritual energy which, after all, is the life within us; that we are not inert dust, nor even transient animals endowed with the ability to think. We must decide that we are "superior energy". That we are spirit.

It's up to us. In a way, we all are unwitting expressions of the universal. So are the stars and galaxies over our heads. So is the dust under our feet. All these react to the indomitable laws. The universal is holy. It is the Whole. We, humans, however, are endowed with free will – a divine gift which we fail to exercise. To do so, a diametric change must take place in our consciousness. Regardless of the promulgation of countless religions, we are what we believe we are. Nothing less, and nothing more. Behind us millions of years of reactive evolution. Ahead – limitless possibilities. Our destiny....

---

[223] The famous equation: $E = MC^2$ illustrates this concept.
[224] "Cogito, ergo sum" from the DISCOURSE ON THE METHOD OF RIGHTLY CONDUCTING THE REASON, René Descartes. [from The Philosophical Works of Descartes]

....for an instant, hovering within an infinite procession of sequential fragments of the divine present, we too might be chosen to become a unit of consciousness through which the Whole finds Its expression. The universal and the particular shall be one. For the sake of a tribe or the whole world. Or perhaps to shed light, beauty or joy on just one other being. These precious moments are known at a subliminal, or perhaps sublime, level to those chosen children of the universe we know as artists. True artists – those who allow their soul to communicate directly with another spiritual entity. Until we earn this privilege, we must learn, gather experience. Perhaps Aristotle was hinting at this, eventual union, when he wrote: "experience is knowledge of particulars, art of universals."[225]

If we are to become artists, let us gather experience...

***
970512

*In an instant,
rise from time and space
Set the world aside and become a world within yourself.*

Shabistari
Secret Garden

---

[225] Aristotle METAPHYSICS, trans. Philip Wheelwright, [The Odyssey press, 1951]

52

BEYOND RELIGION
I

Evolution of consciousness as an individual entity, or Self, is divided into three distinct phases: the kindergarten, the school and the university. Progressively, these phases serve to assert individuality, expand its range of awareness and ultimately pass beyond the inherently assumed limitations.

Phase one: THE KINDERGARTEN.

It begins when the rudimentary consciousness asserts its will to survive as an individual unit. An amoeba, a virus, a bacterium. The mono-cellular entity becomes aware of the inside and the immediate outside of itself. It defines its territory, its boundaries. The primitive consciousness learns the laws of survival by re-embodying itself within ever more complex physical forms. Each re-embodiment is designed to increase the scope of its operations. The Sanskrit scriptures place the number of transmigrations of (each individualization of) consciousness at 8,400,000. Hopefully this number includes the second phase of our evolution, though I doubt it. Suffice to say that the primary stage of our existence consists exclusively of assuring physical survival and well-being.

The learning process in this phase relies on repetitive conditioning. The method is that of trial and error. The repetitions serve to develop a subconscious – a storehouse of information on which the primitive consciousness can draw to survive within its embodiment in ever changing environments. Its responses to challenges are reactive, i.e. automatic or instinctive. There is little evidence of free will or deductive reasoning, although the acquired experience is carefully stored in the genetic code of the biological constructs the entity produces to advance its evolution. At this stage, the individual consciousness is subject to the indomitable laws of nature. A mistake costs it its life.

Phase two: THE SCHOOL.

During this phase the entity develops advanced communication skills and becomes susceptible to the influences of theoretical knowledge. It learns to be selective in its relationship to the universal laws governing its environment. In the school, the teachers are responsible for the efficacy of imparting knowledge to their pupils. During this evolutionary phase, the units of consciousness are organized within a variety of classrooms. The purpose of this tendency towards aggregations is to extend the awareness of the self beyond its space/time confines, i.e.: beyond its physical enclosure. The classrooms consist of groups within which the self reaches out to include the allegiance to families, clans, villages, towns, religious congregations and national formations – with which the Self can identify. The teachers (those in authority), in order to facilitate control over the nascent units of consciousness, endeavour to maintain them in abject ignorance. We are taught that obedience – to those in power – is a virtue. Regrettably, with few exceptions, the teachers are also ignorant of the true reality. The rare avatars (invariably nonconformists and in direct opposition to the prevailing *status quo*) cast seeds of wisdom on the developing states of consciousness. The seeds seldom strike fertile soil. More often than not they meet an inflexible mindset bent on protecting rather than improving acquired knowledge. Other seeds reach receptive minds, but are stifled by the orthodox establishment in control. The few who break with traditions are ridiculed, often persecuted, sometimes killed. Free thought and individuality is strongly discouraged by those wielding power.

The last segment of this phase, is characterized by rebellion. We gradually lose faith in our teachers. We observe countless contradictions between their teaching and their behaviour pattern. This dichotomy is particularly in evidence within the sacerdotal and political ranks. We still obey, mostly due to inbred fear, but simultaneously begin to strike out on our own. This invariably leads to a period of apostasy that results in achieving a degree of freedom from previous conditioning. When we feel secure, we begin to compare the various teachings, each claiming absolute exclusivity over truth. We discover that if we eliminate ninety-nine percent of the miasma that our teachers (leaders, politicians, preachers, priests, parents, elders) have imposed on the *original* teachings, the residual essence is virtually the same. We suspect that if all the great avatars taught the same *a priori* knowledge, then there must be an original source from which they, the avatars, drew their wisdom.

We begin searching for the source.

Phase three: THE UNIVERSITY.[226]

We become students. We discover that our newly found freedom is commensurate with our acceptance of responsibility. We no longer hold teachers, preachers, priests, confessors, psychologists, politicians, mothers or fathers or even circumstances responsible for our survival. In fact, our definition of survival is undergoing a fundamental change. The extension of our physical life is no longer our priority. Quality takes preference over quantity. We begin to suspect, then know that we are entities with an unimaginable potential. We learn from every quarter, from the past and the present, from nature, from the positive and negative traits still integral to our mental, emotional and physical embodiments. We learn the difference between reactive and causative action. We refuse to conform for the sake of the illusion of security we used to derive from the concept of belonging. We become individuals. Tremulously, we step...

BEYOND RELIGION.

Since the preceding phases deal with survival within the constrains of time and space, they are also confined to specific duration. Our university, however, deals with that which has neither beginning nor end. It finds its reality outside the constrains of the space/time continuum. This realization empowers us to step outside our material constrains. Outside our physical bodies. From this new vantage point we observe the forces controlling our environment. We observe the rich becoming richer, the poor – poorer. The happy – increasing in their joy, the miserable sinking into depression. *Regardless of circumstances*. We became aware of the universal rule that, unwittingly, controlled us from the moment we became enwrapped in material reality:

---

[226] From Latin *universitas*, the whole (world), the universe.

WE ARE THE PRODUCT OF OUR CONTEMPLATION.

We note that every thought we entertain influences our environment. Every thought we energize with emotion – defines our future. We learn to control our thoughts. We become selective in the use and learn to control our emotions. We learn that to realize a dream, we must have a dream. To reach a goal, we must have a goal. To realize the impossible, we must believe that everything is possible. We become the conscious effect of the creative power of our beliefs. We perceive that at every instant of existence, we are the consequence of our past, the forerunners of our futures. We take control.

Growing we grow, maturing we mature, ever reaching for the eternally receding horizon. Slowly, so very slowly, it dawns on us that there are no horizons. We realize that we, ourselves, define the characteristics and the scope of our reality. We realize that we create the universe in which we find our being.

The lightening strikes. Time stops. We begin living in the present.

***

Ye are gods

Psalm 82:6

A Word about the Author

Stanislaw Kapuscinski, (aka **Stan I.S. Law**), architect, sculptor and prolific writer was educated in Poland and England. Since 1965 he has resided in Canada. His special interests cover a broad spectrum of arts, sciences and philosophy. His fiction and non-fiction attest to his particular passion for the scope and the development of Human Potential. He authored more than thirty books, twenty of them novels.

Under his real name he published seven non-fiction books sharing his vision of reality. He also composed two collections of poems in his original native tongue in which he satirizes his view of the world while paying homage to Bozena Happach's sculptures.

Finally, he and his wife publish two blogs online, which, to date of this printing have been already visited by hundreds of thousands of people. We both hope you'll enjoy them as much.

Acknowledgments

I would be remiss were I not to thank my many friends for their comments, advice, and proofreading, none more so than Madeleine Witthoeft who's editing raised this book to acceptable literary standards. As always my gratitude to my wife, Bozena Happach, who put up with being a grass widow for weeks on end, and then offered me her inspired insights.

Sincerely,
Stanisław Kapuściński

Smashwords wrote in their Annual Review:

If you write a book that touches your readers' soul, or inspires them with passion or knowledge, your readers will market your book for you.

I've done my part. The rest is up to you.
And if you enjoyed my efforts, please write a (brief) review.
Your thoughts are important to me.

(The covers are, of course, in full colour)

INHOUSEPRESS, MONTREAL, CANADA
email: hap.kap@sympatico.ca